Parents, Kids & Character

21 Strategies To Help Your Children Develop Good Character

by

Dr. Helen R. LeGette

Parents, Kids & Character

21 Strategies To Help Your Children Develop Good Character

by Dr. Helen R. LeGette

CHARACTER DEVELOPMENT PUBLISHING

Phone (919) 967–2110, fax (919) 967–2139

E-mail respect96@aol.com
Cover design by Sara Sanders
Book design by Sara Sanders
Text editing by Ginny Turner
Project director, Ginny Turner

ISBN 1-892056-01-1 $15.95

*To all children & teenagers
and to the adults who
care about them*

CHAPTER

Acknowledgments

I would like to express my heartfelt appreciation to:

Dr. Thomas Lickona, Dr. Henry Huffman, and Dr. Philip Vincent, for their leadership in character education and the ways in which their work and their examples have touched my life.

Dr. Joseph Sinclair, for allowing me to help establish character education as a priority in our schools and in our community.

The many parents, teachers, and administrators whom I have had the privilege of knowing and working with, for reinforcing my belief that most people are good and kind and caring.

The students whom I have taught, counseled, and learned from, for the many ways in which they have inspired and motivated me.

My friends and family members, for their interest in this project and for their words of encouragement when I needed them most.

My parents, for the lives they lived and the examples they provided.

And most of all, my husband Harry, for his support, editing assistance, and unwavering love and encouragement.

CHAPTER

Contents

Introduction

C haracter education and character issues are receiving almost unprecedented attention in the media and in public and private conversations. Thoughtful adults are increasingly concerned about the messages about morality which children and youth are receiving from their peers and from media, political, and sports figures.

In recent months, high-paid and high-profile sports figures have engaged in acts such as spitting in the face of an umpire, striking a photographer, and threatening to kill a basketball coach. When questioned about whether Mike Tyson would be allowed to box again after biting a chunk of flesh from an opponent's ear, one sportscaster thought for a moment and then replied that he believed Tyson would indeed return to the ring. His logic? "Money talks and character walks."

Reports of questionable ethics by politicians in high places and possibly illegal fund-raising by both major political parties fill the newspapers and airwaves. Charges and countercharges break like waves on the shore, and every week seems to bring new allegations against our national leaders. Larry Sabato, professor of government at the University of Virginia, said recently that reports of scandal have become "the elevator music" of American politics because "scandal, like elevator music, is always there in the background."[1]

1

It's been said that we are living in an age of "so what and who cares?" Bumper stickers, banners and t-shirts bombard us with obscene messages. Language which would have been totally unacceptable a generation ago is commonplace today. Far too many young Americans are abusing drugs, engaging in high-risk sexual behavior, and committing shocking acts of violence against others and themselves. They have pitifully few real heroes, and, not surprisingly, some youth confuse being famous with being good.

In national surveys, as many as two-thirds of high school students admit to cheating at some time in school. The belief that cheating is wrong only if you get caught is widespread among our youth. Many subscribe to what Michael Josephson calls the "I Deserve It Creed":

Whatever I want, I need.
Whatever, I need, I deserve.
Whatever I deserve,
I have a right to have,
And I will do anything to get it.[2]

This philosophy manifested itself boldly in a courtroom in my community. A middle school student had been arrested for beating and robbing a peer of twenty dollars. The judge turned to the youngster and asked, "Son, why did you do this?" He replied, "Because he had it and I wanted it." In his mind, the fact that he wanted the other boy's money was reason enough to beat and rob him!

The attitude that only I matter and that life is dispensable is alarmingly widespread. Children and teenagers are killing one another at unprecedented rates. For example, the nation was shocked several years ago when a four-year-old was dropped to his death from a high-rise apartment building in Chicago by two pre-teens. The reason for the crime was that the younger child refused to steal candy for his murderers. In December 1997, a quiet teenager in Paducah, Kentucky, arrived at school heavily armed. He shot into a group of students who were having a before-school prayer session, killing three of his classmates. He told investigators that he was acting out the theme from a movie he had watched.

Social observers fear that some of our young people don't have a conscience, so there is no moral voice guiding their actions. That would seem to be true in several recent incidents. For example, two youths from privileged homes in New Jersey delivered their illegitimate child in a motel room. They then allegedly killed the baby and dumped him in a garbage bin. Soon after that event, another high school student in New Jersey gave birth to a son, deposited him in the trash can, cleaned herself up and returned to the dance floor to enjoy her senior prom. A similar, chilling episode occurred in Greensboro, North Carolina, in January 1997, when a young woman who had hidden her pregnancy from her parents gave birth to a little girl and left her in a dumpster, where the baby died.

How did we reach this point? To answer that question, we need to remember that children are like mirrors, and their lives reflect the world which we adults have created for them. Even when we don't like what we see, we must face the fact that their attitudes and their values are a reflection of direct and indirect lessons they have learned from our society. This sobering thought has prompted politicians, educators, and concerned parents alike to look critically at our current culture.

Serious questions are being raised about the moral direction in which America seems to be heading. Jeffrey Scheler captures the feelings of many Americans in his statement that "the social critics among us, and the consciences within us, increasingly wonder if we have lost our moral compass."[3] Pollster Daniel Yankelovich reports that "moral confusion is widespread and the shared norms that hold our society together are breaking down." He adds that ninety percent of Americans believe that social morality is in a "state of decline and decay."[4] Similarly, nine out of ten Americans polled in 1994 survey commissioned by *U.S. News and World Report* expressed concerns about the moral condition of our nation.[5]

Like Yankelovich, George Gallup has conducted numerous public opinion surveys. In *The Content of America's Character*, Gallup writes: "Americans today are more concerned about the state of morality and ethics in their nation than at any other time in the six decades of scientific polling."[6]

Marian Wright Edelman, president of the Children's Defense Fund, believes that "the greatest threat to our national security and future comes from no external enemy but from the enemy within— in our loss of strong, moral, family, and community values and support."[7] The task of teaching positive values to children is even more difficult, Edelman maintains, when "public figures and advertisers equate drinking with fun and relaxation and glamour; when many television programs and movies seed and feed an apparently insatiable American appetite for gratuitous violence; and when unmarried parents dot the covers of best-selling magazines."[8]

Concerned parents and others who care about children are saddened by the laxity in common courtesy today, especially among our youth. Herbert London, professor of humanities at New York University, states that many well-paid "artists" of the literary and entertainment worlds seem "intent on overturning manners, morals, legitimacy, decency and taste." They believe, says Dr. London, that "rejecting manners is liberating and that coarse language is instructive."[9] Expressing similar concerns, nationally syndicated columnist Walter Williams warns that as older generations die, fewer Americans will even be aware of the decline in moral standards.[10]

Despite the nagging fear that America could be rearing a generation of young people who are morally illiterate, there is also increasing hope that current trends can be reversed. Since the mid-1980s, a quiet movement has been occurring. That movement involves the conscious, cooperative effort of parents, teachers, and religious instructors to teach positive moral values to children and youth through direct instruction and by personal example.

Character education, long a responsibility of three major social institutions—the family, the school, and the church—is re-emerging as a national priority. Still recovering from the 1960s and the 1970s, when a major focus was on *my* rights and *my* needs, and the preoccupation with wealth and greed of the 1980s, more and more Americans are critically examining the messages we are transmitting to our children. School board members, legislators, parents, and educators finally seem to understand that we *must* work together if we are going to bring up young people who are not only academically prepared, but who are also good and caring citizens.

One of the leaders in the character development movement in this country is Michael Josephson, founder of the Josephson Institute of Ethics and the Character Counts! Coalition. He has worked tirelessly to raise consciousness of the character crisis in America. Mr. Josephson cautions against pointing fingers of blame or responsibility at the church, the school, the family, or the government. Although there is plenty of blame to share, it is futile to look for any one source of the moral mess we are in. Rather, we must understand that instilling principles of character (respect, responsibility, fairness, caring, citizenship, and trustworthiness) in our children is both an *obligation* and an *opportunity* for *all* of us.[11]

A starting point for any effort to improve the character of our youth is the realization that good character is not inherited; it must be *taught*. In the home, in the classroom, in religious institutions, and in the community, adults must deliberately and diligently teach what it means to be a person of good character. Only if children hear lessons about moral behavior, see examples of good and ethical conduct, and have an opportunity to put into practice what they have learned will we see a difference in the current moral trends. We adults must face Robert Steinback's very pertinent question: "If virtue isn't universal, is it because some have failed to learn it—or because others have failed to teach it?"[12] George Nicholaw, of KNX Radio in Los Angeles, provides a painful answer when he observes that "children cannot heed a message they have not heard."[13]

The family lies at the heart of any effort to re-focus on character development. Parents are the primary transmitters of values to children, and it is they who bear the major responsibility for teaching by word and example what it means to be a moral person. Thomas Lickona, one of the nation's most respected character education proponents, states that "parents are their children's first moral teachers [and] they are also the most enduring influence."[14]

Because of the moral turbulence of our era, many parents underestimate their influence with their own children. They feel overpowered by the Pied Pipers of media and music their children are following. However, a surprising number of youth, when asked to name the person who has had the greatest impact on their lives, will name a parent. Several recent large-scale studies have confirmed what we knew in our hearts all along: Good family relationships *do* make a difference in the character of children! For example, a study involving approximately 12,000 adolescents revealed that youth who feel a sense of "connectedness" with their parents are less likely to engage in violence, substance abuse, or precocious sexual activity.[15]

It should be encouraging to parents to be reminded that good family life not only lays the foundation for good moral development, but it also increases the likelihood that young people will exhibit good character and be able to resist strong peer influence. Close family relationships give children "people to identify with, examples to learn from, values and traditions to uphold, and a support system to turn to in times of need." Simply put, the family provides "a rudder that helps them hold to a course of responsible conduct even in the face of pressure from friends."[16]

It has been my privilege to work with numerous parents, students, and educators during my career as a teacher, counselor, administrator, and consultant. In those various roles, I have observed that most people *want* to be good. I have taught and counseled many young people who personified caring, compassion, and courtesy. Furthermore, I have known and admired educators and parents who taught good character, not only in their words, but also in the daily living of their lives.

Unfortunately, I have also observed firsthand some of the disturbing behaviors and attitudes highlighted in this introduction. Consequently, I am pleased that so many people are now focused on character issues and are conscientiously trying to make a difference for our children. However, I am convinced that all of these efforts will be far less effective without a serious shoring-up of the family. It is the parents who will make the most profound differences, and it is the parents who have the most challenging work ahead of them.

The twenty-one strategies offered in this book grew out of my work as associate superintendent of a public school system in North

Carolina. In that role, I worked with local parents, educators, board of education members, and representatives of community agencies in planning and implementing a character education project. A group of parents who were trying to ensure that children would be hearing the same kinds of messages about character in the home and at school asked me to provide some recommendations to them. The twenty-one strategies were a part of the resource material that I compiled for them, and the list has been widely shared with educators and parents across the nation.

This book is an elaboration on the original list. It is not intended as a handbook on child development or a recipe for rearing good children. Rather, I hope it will serve as a useful and practical resource for parents to help them in the most important work any of us can do: instilling good character in children and youth. Therein lies the hope of our nation and our world.

[1] Editors, *Chicago Tribune*, "Dulling the Senses: Scandal All the Time," Greensboro (NC) *News and Record* (January 22, 1998), p. A5.

[2] Michael Josephson, *Let's Get Involved: What You Should Know about Character Counts!* [Guide to videotape *Let's Get Involved*] (Marina del Rey, CA: Josephson Institute of Ethics, 1996), p. 11.

[3] Jeffrey Scheler, "Spiritual America," *U. S. News and World Report* (April 4, 1994), p. 48.

[4] Edward F. DeRoche and Mary M. Williams, *Educating Hearts and Minds* (Thousand Oaks, CA: Corwin Press, Inc., 1998), p.1.

[5] Scheler, op. cit., p. 56.

[6] Don E. Eberly, ed., *The Content of America's Character* (Lanham, MD: Madison Books, 1995), p.ix.

[7] Marian Wright Edelman, *The Measure of Our Success* (Boston: Beacon Press, 1992), p. 19.

[8] Ibid., p. 52.

[9] Herbert London, "In America, Bad Behavior Pays Big," Greensboro (NC) *News and Record* (January 25, 1998), p. A5.

[10] Walter Williams, "We Suffer from Moral Decadence," Burlington (NC) *Times News* (November 8, 1997), p. A4.

[11] Josephson, op cit.

[12] Robert L. Steinback, "The Brinks Case Puts Virtue to the Test," Greensboro (NC) *News and Record* (January 17, 1997), p. A6.

[13] David Brooks and Frank G. Goble, *The Case for Character Education* (Northridge, CA: Studio 4 Productions, 1997), p. iv.

[14] Thomas Lickona, *Educating for Character: How Our Schools Can Teach Respect and Responsibility* (New York: Bantam Books, 1992), p. 396.

[15] Michael Resnick et al., "Protecting Adolescents from Harm," *Journal of the American Medical Association* (September 10, 1997), pp. 823-832.

[16] Thomas Lickona, *Raising Good Children* (New York: Bantam Books, 1994), p. 31.

Model good character in the home.

G eneral Colin Powell was one of two children born to Jamaican immigrants Luther and Arie Powell. The elder Powells both worked in the garment district, so Colin and his sister were latchkey children. After school, they sometimes stayed with neighbors or relatives, but often they were on their own. The situation, according to General Powell, could have been a "recipe for trouble."[1]

What was their saving grace? It was the influence of the parents even when they were not physically present. General Powell states that the elder Powells "did not recognize their own strengths." In obvious respect and admiration, he explains that he and his sister learned their early lessons about character not from what their parents said, but from the way they lived their lives. According to General Powell, he and his sister "had been shaped not by preaching, but by example, by moral osmosis."[2]

In a similar manner, the character of Arun Gandhi, founder of the M. K. Gandhi Institute for Nonviolence, was profoundly influenced by his grandfather, Mohandas (Mahatma) Gandhi. He often heard the great proponent of nonviolence speak of the importance of tolerance and respect, and he had ample opportunity to see those qualities in action in his grandfather's life. Arun grew up in South

Africa under apartheid, but he moved to India in 1957. Years later, he had a chance encounter with, and was greeted warmly by, a member of the South African Parliament. Immediately, Gandhi realized that the man was one of the people responsible for the humiliation and prejudice he had experienced in South Africa. Gandhi recalls that, in that split-second, he thought, "Here is the guy who was responsible for all of the humiliation I suffered for 24 years. He is now in my country and in my grasp. I can tell him to jump into the sea, and I can insult him, and I can do whatever I like to him, and nobody is going to question it."[3]

Arun Gandhi stopped that train of thought at once, however, and shifted to the question, "What would grandfather do if I did that?" He quickly realized that any effort at retribution would have been displeasing, not only to his grandfather, but to his father as well. "Instead of showing my anger and getting that revenge," Gandhi said, "I offered a hand in friendship."[4]

Both the Powell and Gandhi families illustrate William Bennett's assertion that "there is nothing more influential, more determinant in a child's life than the moral power of a quiet example."[5] Like General Powell and Arun Gandhi, most of us could probably name a parent or other admired relative who has had a lasting impact on our lives. We would also probably share their observations that it was not so much what those individuals *said* (although overt teaching is important in character development), but what they *did* in the daily living of their lives that made us want to be like them.

Hearing someone say that it is important to be honest is one thing. Seeing that person consistently demonstrate honesty and integrity, possibly at great personal expense, makes a far more lasting impact. Conversely, the parent who tells his children to be respectful of others and then uses ethnic or sexist humor communicates a very powerful negative moral message to them. Similarly, parental lectures about respect for others fall on deaf ears when children are addressed in sarcastic, demeaning ways. Such discrepancies between what we say and what we do can—and almost certainly will—cause moral conflict and confusion for children. In some situations, they might even be unaware of their own wrongdoing.

To illustrate, consider the following story shared by an educator in one of my workshops. On a class field trip, one of the children in her class stole something from the museum gift shop. When confronted, the youngster didn't seem at all concerned and didn't appear to understand that he had done anything wrong. The teacher called the parent for a conference to discuss her concerns about the incident and the child's attitude. The mother became irate and verbally attacked the teacher. "That's not so!" she yelled. "You're just lying about my child. He doesn't steal. I've taught him right from wrong." Within the next two weeks, the teacher read in the local newspaper that that mother had been arrested for shoplifting. Obviously, the mother's words and deeds were sadly out of sync.

We who want children to learn to be good can bombard them with a steady stream of *shoulds* and *oughts*, but it is all too easy for children to forget platitudes or moral abstractions. If they are to take adults' moral instruction seriously, they must be able to see those principles of character lived out in the home. Parents have opportunities to model responsible citizenship and good character in everything they do—in their interactions with their spouse, their children and other family members; in their acts of service and compassion toward others; in their business affairs; and in their conversations. Even seemingly insignificant acts of kindness and thoughtfulness speak volumes about who the parent is and what he or she *really* believes.

In *The Moral Intelligence of Children*, Robert Coles states that "character is ultimately who we are expressed in action, in how we live, in what we do."[6] He reminds us that as children witness our daily lives, they "add up, imitate, [and] file away what they've observed." Later (and sometimes to our surprise), they exhibit the very qualities which we have been trying to teach them. The parents' words and deeds—if they match—provide children with a "character-in-action lesson" which they can see and hear and feel.[7]

The responsibilities and pressures of today's parents are intense and unrelenting. They face the daunting task of raising good children in a culture which often communicates moral messages that directly contradict the lessons they want their children to learn. In some ways, their position is like that of the goalie of a hockey team.[8] The "pucks" of coarseness, violence, and social irresponsibility are flying fast and furiously, and it is increasingly difficult to fend off the numerous negative influences threatening their children.

Today's parents have legitimate worries about the flagrantly negative role models in the entertainment and sports worlds. Addressing such concerns, Leonard Pitts, columnist for the *Miami Herald,* acknowledges that the mass media can indeed "warp a young person's perceptions and ideals." However, he appropriately reminds us that it is the child's parents—not Michael Jordan or the Spice Girls— who sit across the dinner table from that youngster each evening.[9] Although the parents lack the glamour and wealth of such celebrities, they at least have the advantage of continuing personal contact with their children.

Let me emphasize that parents do not have to be perfect. They do, however, need to be real. We all make mistakes, and it is entirely appropriate to let children know that we, too, struggle with issues of character. I have read that in ancient Rome, unscrupulous sculptors would attempt to hide their errors by patching or filling blemishes on their statues with wax. Roman citizens who wanted authentic works of art sought out those sculptors who were known for working *sine cera,* or without wax.[10] Children, especially teenagers, are very sensitive to hypocrisy. They watch us closely to see if we are making a sincere effort to practice what we preach. In their hearts, they must be able to believe that their parents are real, that they are truly *sine cera.*

Children and adolescents desperately need the security of being able to trust the most influential adults in their lives. They need to know that, as they struggle with morally ambiguous issues, there is a steadfast someone who is worthy of emulation, someone they can turn to for advice, for comfort, and for support. Emphasizing the impact of personal example, Rabbi Wayne Dosdick offers these encouraging words to parents: "When you live your ideals, you show your children the importance of your moral choices and the sincerity of your decisions. Your children can then learn to honor their values and to keep the promises they make—responsibly and dependably."[11]

Although it was written almost seventy years ago, the following poem by Edgar Guest serves as an appropriate summary of the importance of authenticity in our relationships with those whom we hope to influence in positive ways.

SERMONS WE SEE

I'd rather see a sermon than hear one any day;

I'd rather one should walk with me than merely show the way.

The eye's a better pupil and more willing than the ear;

Fine counseling is confusing, but example's always clear.

And the best of all the preachers are the men who live their creed,

For to see the good in action is what everybody needs.

I can soon learn how to do it if you'll let me see it done;

I can watch your hands in action, but your tongue too fast may run.

And the lectures you deliver may be very wise and true,

But I'd rather get my lesson by observing what you do;

For I may misunderstand you and the high advice you give,

But there's no misunderstanding how you act and how you live.

[1] Colin Powell, *My American Journey* (New York: Random House, 1995), p. 37.

[2] Ibid.

[3] Arun Gandhi, "Stopping the Violence," Greensboro (NC) *News and Record* (January 25, 1998), p. F5.

[4] Ibid.

5 William Bennett, *The Book of Virtues* (New York: Simon & Schuster, 1993), p. 11.

[6] Robert Coles, *The Moral Intelligence of Children* (New York: Random House), p. 7.

[7] Ibid., p. 131.

[8] Anne Lewis, "Where There's a Will," *Phi Delta Kappan* (February, 1998), p. 420.

[9] Leonard Pitts, "Parents Should Not Need a Prod," Greensboro (NC) *News and Record* (September 6, 1997), p. A5.

[10] Denis Waitley, *The Seeds of Greatness* (New York: Simon & Schuster, 1983), p. 96.

[11] Wayne Dosdick, *The Golden Rules: The Ten Ethical Values Parents Need to Teach Their Children* (San Francisco: Harper Collins Publishers, 1995), p. 166.

Be clear about your values and beliefs. Tell your children where you stand on important issues.

A man I know is highly regarded for his kindness and integrity. Successful in business, he frequently offers others a hand up. He has had a positive influence on many young people. When asked how he developed his own value system, he gives much of the credit to his father. To illustrate, he tells of an incident that occurred when he was a teenager, when his father's beliefs made an indelible impression on him.

At the time, the young man had a part-time job in a little country store which was a forerunner of today's convenience stores. One day the father overheard his son and several of his friends laughing about their occasional raids on the ice cream box when the owner was away from the store. After the friends left, the father confronted his son. "Oh Dad, it's not a big deal. We didn't really take anything. All we did was eat a little ice cream."

"Yes, it *is* a big deal," the father countered quietly. "It is stealing and it's not right." He then told his son to get into the car because they were going to the store owner's home, and the youth was going to have to confess what he had done and pay for the ice cream. After hearing about the youthful thefts, the owner stated that he was sadly disappointed in the young man, whom he had trusted to be responsible for the business in his absence. However, he said that he was not going to fire him—provided that there would be no further dishonesty.

As the father and son were returning home, the embarrassed and angry adolescent said nothing. After a while, the father pulled the car to the side of the road. He put his arm around his sullen son and said in a very gentle voice, "Son, I love you more than life itself, and I love you too much to let you get away with dishonesty. I just love you too much to let you mess up your life like this."

This story, told by my minister, illustrates the importance of parents' making clear statements about their values and letting their children know where they stand on important issues. If the father had laughed with the teenagers or let the incident slip by without comment, the youth would have assumed that petty theft was okay. After all, everybody does it—isn't that the message our youth hear constantly? The older man might have enjoyed a few minutes of being one of his son's pals, but he would have lost an invaluable opportunity to influence his son's character.

In Strategy One we considered the importance of teaching moral lessons through personal example. Some educators and psychologists criticize direct teaching of moral principles, such as citizenship, fairness, and responsibility. Their position is that the only meaningful moral messages are learned from personal examples. They maintain that character is "caught" rather than "taught." However, I believe, as do many other character educators, that character is both caught and taught. It just makes sense that if we want our children to internalize the virtues that we value, we need to teach them what those virtues are. To do that effectively, we need both words and deeds.

Learning about what good character is by watching a worthy role model is invaluable, but personal example alone is not enough. To counter the influence of the bad examples that young people encounter every day, we need to offer them our beliefs as well as our behavior. In *Raising Good Children*, Thomas Lickona states that children need to "see us leading good lives, but they also need to know why we do it." That is, for our personal example to have maximum impact, children need to know what the values are that guide our conduct and decisions. Simply stated, we have to *tell* them what we believe.[1]

Throughout the early history of this nation, moral instruction was a part of every child's life. Parents and teachers took quite seriously their responsibility to teach children right from wrong. Using the Scriptures, mottoes, adages, poems, and books such as the *McGuffey Readers*, the older generation took advantage of many opportunities to instill virtue in children. However, in the social and moral upheavals of the 1960s and succeeding decades, many parents became less deliberate in their moral teaching. Possibly reared by permissive parents themselves, or educated during the height of the values clarification movement, some adults became so afraid of "imposing" their own values on children that they became very nondirective. They abdicated their roles as moral guides and teachers, and the result was a "values vacuum" in the home. To fill that vacuum, the media, advertising, and peer influence rushed in.[2]

As mentioned in the introduction, recent surveys show that nine out of ten of Americans believe that our nation is experiencing a moral crisis. It is not surprising, therefore, that many parents are reassuming their roles as moral teachers. They understand that their most important legacy for their children is a "moral heritage." Such parents realize that each succeeding generation benefits from the set of values passed on by their parents. Those principles of character provide a solid moral foundation for them.[3] Those moral standards or virtues are always a part of us, as William Bennett asserts. They "become a moral compass point, guiding and instructing us for the rest of life's journey."[4]

There are countless ways in which parents can take a meaningful stand in front of their children to increase the capital in that moral heritage. Such stands need not involve preaching or ostentatious orations. The most effective teaching is often done in very ordinary, everyday situations. To illustrate this point, please consider the following incidents:

- A neighbor tells an off-color joke in front of your child and laughs uproariously

- Your child is playing in a Little League game, and the parents all around you are yelling obscenities at the umpire.
- Your teenager is invited to a party at which you suspect alcohol will be served.
- Your daughter tells you that her best friend is having sex with her boyfriend.
- One of your children repeats some hurtful gossip about a neighbor.

In moments such as these, parents have opportunities to let their children know what they believe about respect, premarital sex, substance abuse, and other character issues. Youth struggle with these concerns, and they are easily influenced by their peers. In the midst of the conflicting moral messages bombarding them, it is critical that teenagers hear and recognize the sound of their own parents' voices.

In *Between Parent and Teenager*, Haim Ginott emphasizes adults' responsibility to set standards and demonstrate our beliefs. He says, "Our message to our children should be : 'We value integrity more than popularity. We put personal decency above social success.'"[5] Ginott further maintains that taking a strong stand on values makes a significant impact on teenagers. "Even if they don't like our words, they respect our strength and value our integrity. They derive pride and dignity from our insistence on courage and fairness."[6]

While the major moral conflicts for children come in adolescence, it is absolutely critical that parents not wait until the teen years to start letting their children know what they believe about important issues and why. Robert Coles, who has extensively studied the moral development of children, says that in elementary school, perhaps as never before or after, the child "becomes an intensely moral creature." This "age of conscience" is a critical period when the conscience must be developed, or the opportunity may be forever lost.[7] "Without doubt," Coles maintains, "most elementary school children are not only capable of discerning between right and wrong," but they also are "vastly interested in how to do so."[8]

It is vitally important to capitalize on this early interest in moral behavior. Parents need to lay the foundation for their children to develop an honest and caring conscience during the childhood years, before peer pressures begin to mount. To do so is to give children moral strength when they step onto that emotional roller coaster called adolescence. Obviously, children "who carry a well-formed conscience into their teen years are far better armed to withstand the temptations they'll face than those who graduate from childhood without the benefit of clear moral training."[9]

Raising good children is an arduous task and must be a labor of love, even when the children seem most trying. Experiencing the challenges and frustrations of parenthood himself, Robert Coles once sought counsel from his colleague, the renowned psychiatrist Erik Erikson. What advice did Erikson give to Coles? He said that first, you must know where you stand and then make sure that your kids learn where you stand on important issues, and that they understand why.[10]

The task of developing good character in children requires both patience and day-by-day moral work—work that involves "speaking those moral sentences that you hope your kids will learn from you." If you are successful, says Erikson, you may one day find your own children standing with you, taking a similar position on important issues of character.[11] On that day, you will have reached a major milestone in the moral development of your children.

[1] Thomas Lickona, *Raising Good Children* (New York: Bantam Books, 1994), p. 22.

[2] Ibid., p. 325.

[3] Ibid., pp. 325-326.

[4] William Bennett, *The Book of Virtues* (New York: Simon & Schuster, 1993), p. 20.

[5] Haim Ginott, *Between Parent and Teenager* (New York: The Macmillan Company, 1969), p. 140.

[6] Ibid., p. 141.

[7] Robert Coles, *The Moral Intelligence of Children* (New York: Random House, 1997), p. 98.

[8] Ibid., p. 105.

[9] Lickona, op. cit., p. 188.

[10] Coles, op. cit., p. 194.

[11] Ibid.

Show respect for your spouse, your children, and other family members.

On June 27, 1997, the Greensboro *News and Record* carried an Associated Press story about a poll called "Kids These Days: What Americans Really Think about the Next Generation." Sixty-one percent of the 2,000 adults surveyed said that the failure of children and youth to learn character traits such as honesty, respect, and responsibility is "a serious problem." Of the respondents, only 37 percent felt confident that today's youngsters will grow up to "make the world a better place." The vast majority expressed concerns about youngsters' attitudes, with just 12 percent agreeing that kids usually treat others with respect.

If you were to conduct your own informal survey and ask the typical American adult to list his or her top five concerns about today's youth, the odds are very good that a lack of respect would appear on that list. I have asked this question many times in workshops, and time after time, I have heard the same concerns from educators and parents. Examples often cited include disrespect for parents, for teachers, for those who are older or different, and for authority figures of all descriptions.

A friend who is assistant principal of a middle school shared the following incident. He was conducting a conference with a student and his mother because of the student's having been in a fight at school and having been blatantly insubordinate to a staff member. As she listened to the account of her son's behavior, the mother began to sob. "Son, I don't know what else to do. I've tried so hard." Unmoved by her tears, the youth glared at his mother and snapped, "Why don't you shut up? You're just full of crap!"

The administrator was shocked at the youth's daring to show such a lack of respect for his mother—especially in the presence of another adult. The mother was hurt and humiliated. It's hard to know what the youth was thinking, but one strong possibility is that he would have a story to tell his peer group. He would gain "respect" from them for daring to stand up to his mother and to the assistant principal. Boasting of his boldness, he would add to his own status and acceptance. Unfortunately, stories abound about acts of crime or violence—even including murder—which teenagers have inflicted on other teens or adults whom they perceived as having "dissed" (shown disrespect for) them in some way.

In *Educating for Character*, Thomas Lickona proposes that the schools should add the "fourth and fifth Rs"—*respect* and *responsibility* to the curriculum. Learning these qualities, he believes, is as basic to children's education as is the mastering of reading, writing, and arithmetic. Respect, which Dr. Lickona describes as the very core of morality, "keeps us from hurting what we ought to value."[1] To be respectful is to have respect for ourselves, for other people, and for life in all of its forms, as well as for the environment that sustains life.[2] He goes on to say what we all know: One of the best ways to help children learn to respect themselves and others is to respect them and require respect in return. Simply stated, respect begets respect.

In schools across America, many teachers are and have been incorporating these principles of character into their daily lessons and interactions with children. However, such efforts will have far less impact if children do not hear the same kinds of messages at home. Learning respect in the family prepares children to respect others, and it decreases the likelihood that they will exhibit negative behaviors such as racial, ethnic, age, or sexual prejudices. Obviously, those who have genuine respect for others will not demean them with hateful comments or actions.

For parents to teach respect, the lessons begin with their own behavior and attitudes toward other family members. Despite the many forms which the American family takes, for the majority of couples, it was love for each other that led to the establishment of the home in the first place. Therefore, it seems appropriate for children to look at the way the parents treat each other to understand what both love and respect mean.

Parents who honor each other, who share family responsibilities, and who resolve their differences in peaceful ways communicate a powerful message about respect to their children. As children see evidence of their parents' mutual respect and concern for each other, they learn invaluable lessons about character. At the same time, they internalize values which will affect their relationships with the opposite sex and the eventual establishment of their own homes.

Parents also communicate volumes about respect in the way they treat older family members. "The Old Grandfather and the Grandson," by Leo Tolstoy, illustrates this point in a powerful way:

> The grandfather had become very old. His legs wouldn't go, his eyes didn't see, his ears didn't hear, he had no teeth. And when he ate, the food dripped from his mouth.
>
> The son and daughter-in-law stopped setting a place for him at the table and gave him supper in back of the stove. Once they brought dinner down to him in a cup. The old man wanted to move the cup and dropped and broke it. The daughter-in-law began to grumble at the old man for spoiling everything in the house and breaking the cups and said that she would give him dinner in a dishpan. The old man only sighed and said nothing.
>
> Once the husband and wife were staying at home and watching their small son playing on the floor with some wooden planks: he was building something. The father asked: "What is that you are doing, Misha?" And Misha said: "Dear Father, I am making a dishpan. So that when you and mother become old you may be fed from this dishpan."

The husband and wife looked at one another and began to weep. They became ashamed of so offending the old man, and from then on seated him at the table and waited on him.[3]

In their relationships with their children, parents can model respect through their language, their patience, and their acceptance of their children. Speaking to children in what Thomas Lickona calls "the language of respect" demonstrates to the children that the parent values them and their opinions. At the same time, it helps to build the children's self-respect. Conversely, those who hear only sarcasm and criticism from their parents will doubt their own worth. Such children are more likely to seek respect in negative ways, either in the home or in the community.

Recently, I was about to enter a drugstore when I heard a loud voice. When I got inside, I saw a woman and two small children—one still in a stroller and the other about four years old. The older child was apparently tired and the mother was frustrated. She was literally screaming at the child: "No, we're not going to McDonald's! No, you're not going to get anything else! You've already got a computer. Drag it out of the drawer and play with that!" The child was making replies, but they were very soft. The conversation continued, and the mother's voice became even louder. Adults in the checkout line exchanged embarrassed looks, but the mother seemed unaware of the spectacle she was creating or the messages she was sending to her child. One day, when the child speaks to her in those same tones, she might wonder how he became so disrespectful.

In "Free the Children—They Need Room to Grow," John Holt wrote in 1977:

> At its very best, the family can be . . . an island of acceptance and love in the midst of a harsh world. But too often family members take out on each other all the pain and frustration of their lives that they don't dare take out on anyone else. Instead of being a ready-made source of friends, the family is too often . . . the place where the cruelest words are spoken.[4]

At the end of the day, parents and children often return home tired and frustrated. I have heard that the first five minutes that a family spends together when they are reunited in the evening sets the tone for the family's interactions. Therefore, its seems worthwhile to make a deliberate effort to ensure that those first interactions are positive. The Biblical principle that "a soft answer turneth away wrath" certainly has application here! A few carefully chosen words of kindness and understanding can transform the emotional atmosphere for the family.

Verbal expression is just one form of communication. Listening is another aspect of communication, and there is no more meaningful message of respect than to give someone our undivided attention. I recently realized that someone who was hard of hearing was the best listener I have ever known. She was my mother. Whenever any of her adult children stopped by her home for a visit, she always led us straight into the kitchen, where we shared coffee or tea and some dessert she had made. She would take her seat across the table from us and ask about our lives—how we felt, what we were doing, or how things were going at work. She would focus on our faces as she tried to hear every word, and she often sensed and responded to emotions we did not express in words. Her concern and interest were almost palpable, and she extended the same courtesy to her grandchildren as they became old enough to share their interests with her. Although she was unversed in psychology or human development, my mother modeled the following suggestions for listening to children's concerns which Thomas Lickona advocates:[5]

LISTEN WITH YOUR WHOLE SELF. Often, in the busy-ness of our lives, we half-listen as we think about something else—what happened at work today, what we're going to cook for dinner, or how we're going to meet our family's financial obligations. To listen with our whole selves requires focusing on what the child is saying and maintaining eye contact.

DON'T INTERRUPT CONSTANTLY WITH QUESTIONS AND COMMENTS. We don't like to be interrupted as we express feelings or concerns. Yet, we often cut children off before they can finish what they are trying to tell us, or we interject our own opinions without honoring the child's thoughts.

IF YOU CAN'T LISTEN NOW, SET A TIME WHEN YOU CAN. Sometimes a child will try to tell you something when you really can't stop to listen intently. If that happens, it is important to communicate that both your child and his or her concerns are important to you. Try to set a time when you *can* talk and then be sure to keep that commitment.

ACKNOWLEDGE FEELINGS. Imagine for a moment that one of your best friends discusses a personal problem with you. It is obvious that the situation is emotionally charged and your friend is visibly upset. Would you respond with any of the following comments?

> "That really doesn't matter. I don't know what you're so upset about."
> "If you had a *real* problem, you'd know what it is to be upset."
> "I wish I didn't have any more to worry about than that."
> "Why don't you just grow up?"

Most of us wouldn't dream of disregarding another adult's feelings in so callous a fashion. Yet, we often do that to children. It is an act of love and respect to respond to a child's concerns with patience and sensitivity, acknowledging the emotions that lie behind those concerns. All of us—even in times of fatigue and frustration—need to remember that a child's feelings are just as intense as those of an adult, and their worries are just as real.

My sister-in-law taught in an elementary school where the principal was highly respected by students and staff members. When I asked her what she viewed as the secret of the administrator's success, she said, "She listens." My sister-in-law went on to say that the principal took seriously *any* complaint or concern, regardless of the age or position of the person. For example, a kindergartner who approached the principal with a problem was invited into the principal's office and treated with the same respect afforded to a teacher, a parent or a board of education member. That educator was teaching some very powerful lessons about respect to her students and staff.

To affirm children's worth and to treat them with the ultimate respect is to do what Steven Covey calls viewing them through "the eye of faith."[6] That is, we see in the young not just what they are, but what they may become. To illustrate, consider the following story attributed to Leslie Whitehead: A ragged and unkempt man spent his days begging outside an artist's studio. Observing the beggar from his window, the artist painted the man's portrait and then invited him in to see it. The beggar—who did not recognize himself—asked, "Who is it?" Then, after studying the portrait at some length, he wondered aloud, "Could that be me?" The artist smiled and said gently, "That is the man as I saw him." After a long pause, the beggar straightened his shoulders, lifted his head, and declared, "If that is the man you see, that is the man I will be."

Home is where children learn their most lasting lessons about what it means to be a person of good character. In the daily interactions within the family, parents have countless opportunities to shape their children's attitudes, beliefs, and behaviors. The following poem by an unknown author has been widely circulated. It serves as an appropriate summary of this chapter.

CHILDREN LEARN WHAT THEY LIVE

> If a child lives with criticism,
>   He learns to condemn.
> If a child lives with hostility,
>   He learns to fight.
> If a child lives with ridicule,
>   He learns to be shy.
> If a child lives with shame,
>   He learns to feel guilty.
> If a child lives with tolerance,
>   He learns to be patient.
> If a child lives with encouragement,
>   He learns confidence.
> If a child lives with praise,
>   He learns to appreciate.
> If a child lives with fairness,
>   He learns justice.
> If a child lives with security,

He learns to have faith.
If a child lives with approval,
He learns to like himself.
If a child lives with acceptance and friendship,
He learns to find love in the world.

[1] Thomas Lickona, *Educating for Character: How Our Schools Can Teach Respect and Responsibility* (New York: Bantam Books, 1992), p. 67.

[2] Thomas Lickona, *Raising Good Children* (New York: Bantam Books, 1994), p. 9.

[3] Robert Coles, *The Moral Intelligence of Children* (New York: Random House, 1997), pp. 10-11.

[4] Lickona, *Raising Good Children*, op. cit., p. 270.

[5] Lickona, op. cit., pp. 265-266.

[6] Stephen Covey, *Principle-Centered Leadership* (New York: Simon & Schuster, 1992), p. 59.

Model and teach your children good manners. Insist that *all* family members use good manners at home.

I*f others talk at table be attentive but talk not with meat in your mouth."* This is one of the 110 rules for civil behavior that George Washington carefully copied into a notebook when he was fourteen years old. It is not clear who provided these "Rules of Civility & Decent Behavior in Company and Conversation" to the youth who would become the first president of our nation. It is possible that his father, an older stepbrother or other mentor passed them along to him.

Regardless of how George acquired the rules, it is obvious that he applied them in his life, and they served him well. Despite Washington's humble beginnings, he moved with ease even in the highest levels of society. He was known for his gracious, kind, and courtly manner. After he had been President of the United States for seven years, a foreign diplomat's wife wrote that he "had perfect good breeding, & correct knowledge of even the etiquette of court." But how he acquired it, she added, "heaven knows."[1]

Although many of the 110 rules Washington learned so well had to do with the etiquette of the day, they also addressed moral issues. Rule #1, for example, states that *"every action done in company ought to be done with some sign of respect for those who are present."* That serves not only as an appropriate starting point for learning appropriate behavior, but its focus on respect serves as a succinct summary of what good manners are all about.

The final rule is a direct moral admonition to "labor to keep alive in your breast that little spark of celestial fire called conscience." The composite effect of the rules is to remind the young that they should always be aware of other people and their feelings, remembering that everyone is entitled to respect and consideration, regardless of their social class or position. As we attempt to teach and model good manners for children and youth, our hope is that such civility will—as it did for Washington—become second nature for them.

As a nation, we have neglected the direct teaching of good manners, especially over the past thirty years. There are a number of possible explanations, including the public challenging of authority and the demonstrations of the 1960s. Some believe that the unruly protests of the Vietnam era legitimized rude behavior. Others would say that our more casual dress, lifestyles, and behavior in general have contributed to the demise of even simple social courtesies. As Thomas Lickona says, "somewhere along the way, people got it into their head that manners weren't important. So they stopped stressing good manners with their children and stopped practicing good manners themselves." They lost sight of the principle that "manners are morals," and that they are significant symbols of respect for others.[2]

Regardless of the cause for the decline in manners, there is now an increasing awareness on the part of Americans that we need to return to a kinder, gentler way of relating to one another. Motivated by the bottom line, the corporate world has begun providing formal classes in etiquette to their up-and-coming professionals. Why? According to manners consultant June Hines Moore, some of the young businessmen and -women were "so socially inept they threatened the balance sheet." Because these highly skilled, well-educated young executives "chewed gum, neglected to introduce people, and stuffed their mouths with food while they tried to make the big sale over lunch with a client," corporations began hiring etiquette trainers to smooth off the rough edges.[3]

Whether the issue is courtesy or other simple social graces, it is in the home that good manners have their roots. Just as children do not inherit good character, they do not inherit good manners. They must be taught, and as Dr. Lickona reminds us, manners "will become important to children only if they are important to their parents."[4] Therefore, parents need to start emphasizing even to very young children that basic good manners and common courtesies are expected in the home.

From the time children are able to speak, most parents begin encouraging them to say "please" and "thank you." As the children get a little older, there are opportunities to teach the importance of taking turns and sharing with others, as well as having good table manners. Writing thank-you notes, maintaining eye contact and shaking hands when introduced, and answering the telephone courteously are among the more obvious forms of polite behavior. More important and more subtle, however, are the manners that relate to kindness and consideration.

In *The New Emily Post's Etiquette*, Elizabeth Post reminds us that "all good manners are based on thoughtfulness of others, and if everyone lived by the Golden Rule—do unto others as you would have others do unto you—there would be no bad manners in the world." She adds that etiquette is really consideration for others.[5]

June Hines Moore, who serves as a consultant for business and also teaches manners classes for children, makes a distinction between *etiquette* and *good manners*. "Etiquette," she says, is a "set of rules we memorize." Manners, on the other hand, are much more than a set of rules.[6] "They express how much we care about other people, their feelings, and their needs." According to Mrs. Moore, good manners bring order to our world. They are "under our control because they flow from the heart," and they "give us the power to treat other people with kindness and respect, even when we don't feel like it." Because they involve self-restraint and concern for others, manners are really a matter of character.[7]

In the home and in the school, children's learning good manners is related to their understanding of expectations. To illustrate, consider the following: At the 1996 Character Education Conference in St. Louis, Dr. David Brooks told about a middle school that had a serious problem with student profanity. In the hallways, in the cafeteria, and on school grounds, the young adolescents felt quite free to use language which was inappropriate, to say the least. Reprimands and other punishments had not made any impact on the problem. The faculty members were quite distressed and wanted to change the school climate.

Finally, after much discussion and also talking with a consultant, the teachers agreed that they would no longer react by sending children to the office or suspending them for using profanity. Instead, every staff member would assume responsibility for approaching any child who used profanity and saying simply, "In this school, we don't talk like that."

Within a matter of just a few weeks, the profanity had almost ceased. Imagine the staff's pride when they heard students confront newcomers who cursed, saying to them, "In this school, we don't talk like that."

The same kind of success can occur in the home when parents establish a climate of respect and good manners—even in informal situations. We can establish a climate in our homes in which children learn through our words and our example. For example, parents can say, "In this family, we don't use profanity, verbally abuse one another, or treat one another with disrespect." Wayne Dosdick captures the heart of modeling when he tells parents that when they "speak gentle words," and when they "act out of goodness, kindness, and decency," they create positive memories for their children—"memories on which they will build and sustain their lives."[8]

Even for the most conscientious parents, however, raising well-mannered children is made more difficult today because of the culture in which we live. Children are bombarded with examples of crude behavior and coarse language. On television and in the movies, "cool" young stars get laughs and large salaries for being sarcastic or obscene, and some professional athletes flagrantly flaunt their bad behavior, on and off the field. At college athletic events, fans taunt opposing teams, and even youth league games are not immune from such behavior. As an example, a reader recently wrote to "Dear Abby" about conduct she had observed at her niece's sixth-grade basketball game at the YMCA.

The writer said that parents of the opposing team yelled at her niece (and presumably other players on that team), cheering and jeering each time she missed a basket. Three of the children on that team were reduced to tears during the game because of the rude treatment they received. (Please note that the bad manners were shown by the *adults*, not the children.) These parents were not only setting a terrible example for their own children and for other children who witnessed their behavior, but they were also engaging in unconscionable humiliation of a group of young girls at a very vulnerable stage of their lives.

We could take some comfort if we believed that this was an isolated incident, but all of us have probably witnessed similar outbursts first-hand. Stories are rampant about Little League parents who are abusive to the coaches when their children don't get enough game time. On the other hand, there are coaches of children's teams who model and teach the concept that the goal is to win at all costs. As an illustration, consider the following tirade delivered to a Peewee football team by its coach:

> "You're all a bunch of wimps and sissies! . . . .You hit like a bunch of girls! Are you girls? You, Waldorf! Are you a girl? Answer me Waldorf! Are you a girl? Well then, what's the matter with you out there? Are you afraid you might get hurt? Don't start crying, Waldorf, 'cause I've got no sympathy for that kind of sissy stuff."[9]

In shopping malls, in restaurants, and on the telephone, we encounter rudeness. Even our highways have become unsafe as the latest breach of manners shows itself as "road rage." It seems that the personalities of many Americans change when they get behind the wheel of a motor vehicle. *Time* magazine recently gave the following account of a 40-year-old mother of three whom they called

"Anne." Running behind schedule and rushing to get to her daughter's game, she blasts her horn and admits, "I'm not even thinking of other cars." An older driver slows at an intersection where there is no traffic light. Anne swears and swerves around him. Getting caught up in the emotion, her children shout, "Make him move over," as Anne tailgates a driver in the fast lane. She flashes her headlights, the other driver moves over, and Anne races toward her destination. At one point, she exclaims, "I almost hit that woman," but then she adds that although she isn't an aggressive driver, "there are a lot of bad drivers out there."[10]

Like Anne, most adults would not readily admit to being rude or manifesting poor manners on the road or elsewhere. However, all of us need to be aware not only of the safety issues involved, but of the inappropriate behavior we are modeling for children and teenagers. We are communicating to them that it is acceptable to be rude, angry, and out of control, especially when driving. This point was literally brought home recently to a Cleveland couple who bought their three-year-old a ride-in car. Imagine their shock and dismay as they watched their little girl take her new vehicle out for a spin. What was she doing? She was pounding the horn and shouting, "Damn it! Damn it!"[11]

Psychiatrist John Larson says that road rage—the use of a car as a weapon—is a symptom of a larger problem in our culture: a general lack of tolerance for those who are different from us, "whether in opinion, looks, or driving style." He goes on to say that the "goal is to get there fast and first, to be 'No. 1' at any cost. And being No. 1 has replaced the Golden Rule, or concern for others, as a guiding moral principle."[12] The message, I believe, is obvious. We all need to literally slow down and reconsider the lessons that we want our children to learn versus the messages that we are actually communicating through our behavior and our expectations.

It is easier to teach children table manners and other basic etiquette than it is to teach truly good manners. To do the latter requires a tremendous amount of patience and perseverance. However, making sure that children have numerous opportunities to see their parents and others exhibit courtesy, respect, and kindness can have a subtle and lasting effect, even when we aren't aware that we are teaching.

George Bernard Shaw's play *Pygmalion* (1912), which was adapted into a Broadway musical and movie as *My Fair Lady*, serves as a powerful reminder of the impact of personal example in teaching good manners. In the drama, Professor Henry Higgins, who is a linguist, makes a bet that he can take a common girl (Eliza Doolitttle) from the streets of London and pass her off as a lady in English society. He proposes to do that within three months by teaching Eliza the speech patterns and the etiquette of the upper class of that era. His friend and house guest, Colonel Pickering, accepts the bet and agrees to pay all of the expenses if Higgins succeeds.

Professor Higgins spends long hours every day, working relentlessly to eradicate Eliza's lower-class Cockney speech patterns and honing her social skills. He does indeed successfully present her to "polite" society as a duchess, and he is exultant about the success of his "experiment." However, the professor completely ignores Eliza's feelings, and he fails to see that the success was a result of Eliza's efforts as much as his own.

Professor Higgins was Eliza's formal teacher, but it was from Colonel Pickering that she learned her most valuable lessons and to whom she felt most grateful—not because he paid for her fine new clothes—but because he treated her as a lady, even when she didn't speak or dress like one. She says to the Colonel:

> "It was from you that I learned really nice manners, and that's what makes one a lady, isn't it? You see it was so very difficult for me with the example of Professor Higgins always before me. I was brought up to be just like him, unable to control myself, and using bad language on the slightest provocation. And I should never have known that ladies and gentlemen didn't behave like that if you hadn't been there."[13]

Eliza goes on to say that learning the rules of etiquette and the appropriate speech patterns was similar to learning to dance—simply learning the proper steps and nothing more. However, her real education began when Colonel Pickering extended her the courtesy of calling her "Miss Doolitttle" when they first met. (Higgins, on the other hand, had treated her as a common girl who was beneath him.) Elaborating, Eliza states that the incident was the beginning of self-respect for her:

> "There were a hundred little things you never noticed, because they came naturally to you. Things about standing up and taking off your hat, and opening doors. . . . things that showed you thought and felt about me as if I were something other than a scullery maid; though of course I know you would have been just the same to a scullery maid if she had been let into the drawing room. . . . You see, really and truly, apart from the things anyone can pick up (the dressing and the proper way of speaking, and so on), the difference between a lady and a flower girl is not how she behaves, but how she's treated."[14]

In the English society into which Eliza Doolittle was introduced, knowing the code of behavior to which the upper class subscribed was considered proof of good breeding. Professor Higgins knew the social protocol and was able to impart it to his pupil. However, it was Colonel Pickering who modeled and taught the manners that reflect good character: consideration, respect, and thoughtfulness.

The contrast between Colonel Pickering and Professor Higgins highlights the difference between knowing proper etiquette and having truly good manners. As we consider children's character development, our major concern is not just with knowing which fork to use at a formal dinner. Rather, we want to help them develop the respect for and thoughtfulness of others that lie at the heart of good manners. A worthy goal is to instill in them the ideal of the Golden Rule—which, after all, is manners in action.

[1] Richard Brookhiser, *Rules of Civility: The 110 Precepts that Guided Our First President in War and Peace* (New York: The Free Press, 1997), pp. 1-2.

[2] Thomas Lickona, *Raising Good Children* (New York: Bantam Books, 1994), p. 84.

[3] June Hines Moore, *You Can Raise a Well-Mannered Child* (Nashville, TN: Broadman & Holman Press, 1996), pp. 6-7.

[4] Thomas Lickona, *Raising Good Children* (New York: Bantam Books, 1994), p. 84.

[5] Elizabeth Post, *The New Emily Post's Etiquette* (New York: Thomas Y. Crowell, 1975), p. v.

[6] Moore, *op.cit.*, p.ix.

[7] Ibid.

[8] Wayne Dosdick, *Golden Rules: The Ten Ethical Values Parents Need to Teach Their Children* (San Francisco: Harper Collins Publishers, 1995), p.199.

[9] John Rosemond, *Six-Point Plan for Raising Happy, Healthy Children* (Kansas City: Andrews & McNeel, 1997), p.150.

[10] Andrew Ferguson, "Road Rage," *TIME*, January 12, 1998, p. 68.

[11] Sheryl Harris," Get off My Tail, You Moron! Becoming Anthem of the Road," *Knight Ridder Newspapers*, reprinted in Greensboro (NC) *News and Record*, February, 18, 1998.

[12] Ibid.

[13] George Bernard Shaw, *Pygmalion* in *Adventures in English Literature*, ed. By R. B. Inglis and J. Spear (New York: Harcourt, Brace & Company, 1958), Act V, p. 762.

[14] Ibid.

Have family meals together *without television* as often as possible.

D o you remember TV dinners? Popular in the 1950s and 1960s, these frozen dinners were not particularly tasty or nutritious, but they provided a convenient way for working mothers to provide hot meals for their families. The handy foil trays held a complete meal and could simply be tossed into the trash when the meal was over. Beyond convenience, though, TV dinners were designed to allow family members to eat in front of the television set, and lightweight, portable tables, called TV trays provided chair-side resting places for TV dinners and beverages. With these "modern" innovations, families were no longer restricted to the kitchen for their meals, and the family meal—an important element of family cohesiveness—began a decline from which it has not recovered.

Today, the television set is on during meals in many homes—as it was during those early TV dinners and the result is that very limited meaningful conversation occurs between parents and their children. Family members may be physically together, but there is little interaction if everyone is focused on the six o'clock news or some other program. As a result, everyone misses out on an important opportunity to build and nourish strong family ties.

Aside from the intrusion of the ever-present media, it has become increasingly difficult for today's families to find time to sit down together for shared meals. Work schedules, practices, lessons, meetings, and other appointments all militate against parents' being able to get everyone together at the same time. Yet, this very "busy-ness" is one of the most compelling reasons to place a high priority on eating together as a family as often as possible. Some families set aside certain times such as "Friday Family Nights," Saturday breakfasts, or special Sunday lunches as occasions which *all* members are expected to reserve for family meals. They seem to understand that the family dining table is, as June H. Moore maintains, "one of the few warm places left that we can go to in our high-tech surroundings."[1]

In light of the many competing voices which are communicating values to today's children and youth, the parents' influence becomes even more critical. Thomas Lickona states that much of what is "involved in raising good children is communication." He adds that food can be a "good facilitator of good communication."[2] Because conversation often flows more freely when we are involved in a shared activity, the family meal provides an excellent time for parents and children to discuss ideas and values. Even ordinary acts, such as setting the table, helping to prepare a meal, or cleaning up after dinner can help to reinforce family ties. Whether the meal is a home-cooked feast, a simple sandwich, or fast food hurriedly grabbed at a drive-through, the most important ingredient is the sharing time—the time set aside to reinforce a sense of belonging to and being cared about by the family.

Strong family ties have a significant effect on children's character development and on their academic achievement as well. Two recent research projects offer support for the significance of family life, and especially family meals. The first study, commissioned by *Reader's Digest* in 1994, involved 2,130 high school students. The students took an academic test consisting of 40 questions selected from the National Assessment of Educational Progress, and they also responded to questions about their lives, their values and their families.

When the researchers analyzed the results, they found that students who had close relationships with their families performed at higher levels on the academic test. Although factors such as parents' educational levels and expectations for their children were related to the students' academic scores, the *one* factor which seemed to make the most difference—even more than having both parents in the home—was having family meals together. (The study revealed that 60 percent of those students who reported that their whole family sat around the table for a meal at least four times each week made high academic scores, as compared with only 42 percent of those whose families shared three or fewer meals per week.)[3]

An even more extensive, long-term study of adolescents which further verified the importance of close family ties and shared meals was reported in the September 10, 1997 issue of the *Journal of the American Medical Association.* This research project, which involved almost 12,000 youth, revealed that adolescents who felt love and warmth from their parents and other family members were less likely to engage in high-risk behavior, such as substance abuse (tobacco, drugs, and alcohol) or premarital sex. Not surprisingly, researchers found that the presence of parents at key times of the day, *including mealtimes*, helped to protect young people from these harmful behaviors.[4]

Why do family meals make a difference? Chester E. Finn, a highly respected educator, speculates that mealtime is an excellent time for parents to ask about what their children are doing in school and to communicate their expectations. In some families, both parents live in the home, but they spend very little time with their children. Genuine "connectedness" goes beyond mere presence. Sitting down together for shared meals and shared conversation means that the family does more than simply exist; the members are involved in each others' lives in meaningful ways.[5]

Thomas Lickona advises parents to think of mealtime as "an opportunity to be in touch with kids about all sorts of things, moral matters included."[6] Family meals are a good time to talk about current happenings, not only at home, but also in school and in the community. As children describe their day's experiences, parents have an excellent opportunity not only to hear concerns, but also to share their own ideas and beliefs. Whether the topic is a problem in kindergarten, boy-girl relationships, drug use in schools, or the current political scene, family members have an opportunity to think through important issues with those to whom they matter the most. Children can learn ways to deal with their own moral dilemmas; at the same time, they can understand that their parents also struggle with issues of character.

Although in most families, there is no shortage of conversation material, Dr. Lickona suggests that carefully selected letters to advice columnists such as "Dear Abby" can stimulate moral reasoning. If sensitively discussed, they can "expand children's and adolescents' awareness of the many kinds of problems people have and help them become a little more understanding and sympathetic toward others."[7] Parents and children can join together in analyzing the situations and offering possible solutions. As family members share their ideas, they have opportunities to develop appreciation for opinions that are different from their own. They also can learn to resolve differences and to show respect for other family members.

To counteract the "I deserve it" mentality of our age, parents are faced with the challenge of fostering in their children an attitude of appreciation and thankfulness—a critical component of good character. One way to build and strengthen such an attitude is to begin meals with a blessing or other expression of thankfulness. (The simple act of holding hands around the table while saying grace symbolically expresses a bond with other family members.) Some families choose to begin their meals with a single-sentence "I'm thankful for . . ." statement by each member, including the very young. Parents are often surprised at and touched by the insights of their children at such times.

Another approach is to involve family members in an activity such as the "thankfulness exercise" developed by teacher and author Hal Urban. Dr. Urban uses this activity to help his high school students develop a sense of gratitude. He asks that they write "I'm thankful for" across the top of a sheet of paper and then divide the lower portion of the page into three columns labeled "Things,"

"People," and "Other." After having the students to write down what they are thankful for in each of the three categories, he assigns to them the task of reading their lists four times during the next 24 hours—after lunch, after dinner, at bedtime, and again the next morning before school. He states that there is a dramatic difference in his students' body language and attitudes as they come to class the next day. The reason for the change? To use Dr. Urban's words, "thankfulness does wonders for the soul."[8] While this activity has an impressive impact on a high school class, it would have even greater meaning when shared around the family dinner table.

Parents set the tone for family meals and the sharing that occurs there. The important thing is to establish a climate that says to the children that adult family members value their thoughts and their feelings. Such occasions provide a wonderful opportunity for the family to jointly celebrate even small victories and joys of the day. They also offer a time when members can discuss their disappointments and frustrations within the safety and security of the family circle. Such times provide "a golden opportunity for the kind of family communication that draws kids out, deepens relationships, and makes a difference in their moral development."[9]

In all cultures, food and drink are associated with significant social relationships. Some primitive societies, for example, use the expression "We eat together" to mean that they have a cordial relationship with those who live in another village. In our own culture, major life events are commemorated with some type of communal meal. Families gather to celebrate weddings and the births and baptisms of new babies. When someone dies, friends bring food as an expression of sympathy and concern, and for graduations, bar mitzvahs, and birthdays, a special meal is usually shared by families and friends. These occasions remind us that the events which affect individual members are also significant for the family and community as a whole. They are symbolic expressions that those involved matter and belong to the larger group.

In many ways, the kitchen is the "heart" of the home. It is there that family members gather at the important times of their lives, and it is there that children and adults can join together in some of their most meaningful interactions, especially as related to character issues. Regardless of the degree of formality or what the family discusses at meal time, "civil conversation—listening with respect, asking a question that shows interest in another, sharing honestly and tactfully one's thoughts and feelings—is itself a lived moral experience, and a vital part of a child's moral development."[10]

In addition to providing opportunities to teach and learn important lessons about manners and morals, meals which are prepared and shared with love and mutual respect strengthen family ties. With just a little extra thought and effort, we can use them to bring to life the thoughts expressed by an unknown author in *Love Adds a Little Chocolate*:

> A house is a house—until love comes through the door. . . .And love intuitively goes around sprinkling that special brand of angel dust that transforms a house into a very special home for very special people: your family. Money. . . can build a charming house, but only love can furnish it with a feeling of home. . . . Duty can pack an adequate sack lunch, but love may decide to enclose a little love note inside. . . . Obligation can cook a meal, but love embellishes it with a potted ivy trailing around slender candles. . . . Compulsion keeps a sparkling house. But love and prayer stand a better chance of producing a happy family. Duty gets offended quickly if it isn't appreciated, but love learns to laugh a lot and to work for the sheer joy of doing it. . . . Obligation can pour a glass of milk, but quite often, love adds a little chocolate.[11]

[1] June Hines Moore, *You Can Raise a Well-Mannered Child* (Nashville, TN: Broadman & Holman Press, 1996), p. 110.

[2] Thomas Lickona, *Raising Good Children* (New York: Bantam Books, 1994), pp. 251,254.

[3] Rachel Wildavsky, "What's Behind Success in School?" *Reader's Digest*, October, 1994, pp. 49-55.

[4] Michael Resnick, et al., "Protecting Adolescents from Harm," *Journal of the American Medical Association*, September 10, 1997, pp. 823-832.

[5] Wildavsky, op. cit., pp. 51-52.

[6] Lickona, op. cit., p. 263.

[7] Ibid., p. 417.

[8] Hal Urban, *20 Things I Want My Kids to Know* (Nashville, TN: Thomas Nelson Publishers, 1992), pp.63-65.

[9] Lickona, op. cit., p. 258.

[10] Ibid., p. 263.

[11] Medard Laz, *Love Adds a Little Chocolate* (Ann Arbor, MI: Servant Publications, 1997), p. 15.

Plan as many family activities as possible. Involve your children in the planning.

A father sat on a bench in the park, watching as his son Todd played on the swings. Looking at his watch, he asked the child if he were ready to go home. Todd asked, "Just five minutes, Dad. Please?" More time passed, and the father again called to his son, telling him it was time to go. Once again, the boy pleaded, "five more minutes, Dad. Just five more minutes." Smiling, the father agreed once more.

A woman who was sitting nearby while her own child played on the slide complimented the man for being such a patient father. After a pause, the man explained that his older son Tommy had been killed by a drunk driver while riding his bicycle. Then he added, "I never spent much time with Tommy and now I'd give anything for just five more minutes with him. I've vowed not to make the same mistake with Todd. He thinks *he* has five more minutes to swing. The truth is, I get five more minutes to watch him play."[1]

This vignette illustrates Emily Dickinson's observation: "*That it will never come again/ is what makes life so sweet.*" Children grow up all too soon, and the opportunities to enjoy and to mold them pass quickly. Many modern parents are torn in a constant tug-of-war between the marketplace and the home. Caught up in the desire to provide more and more material comforts for their families, they often sacrifice family time to accumulate additional things, some of which they don't really need. Robert Coles says that many parents are not as involved in their children's lives as were previous generations of parents because they are "too busy spending their most precious capital—their time and energy—struggling to keep up with the MasterCard payments."[2]

Minister and best-selling author Max Lucado receives numerous requests for speaking engagements around the world. As the requests arrive, he places them all in a folder labeled "Decision File." Each June, he puts his calendar together for the next year. One year, as he sifted through the file and reviewed some very flattering offers, he noticed a picture lying on his desk next to folder. It was a photograph of himself, his wife, and their three daughters. Although he had unintentionally placed the portrait next to the stack of requests, he immediately recognized his unconscious intention. The picture, he said, "seemed to whisper a question that only I could answer: 'Max, who will win?'"[3]

The quandary faced by this busy father is all too familiar to today's parents. In addition to career demands, there are requests to serve on committees in the PTA, the church, civic organizations, political campaigns—and the list goes on. On one side, various groups are clamoring for your time and energy. These requests are flattering, they are usually good and noble, and they provide opportunities to serve the larger community. As Reverend Lucado observes, "If they were evil, it would be easy to say no. But they aren't, so it's easy to rationalize."[4]

On the other side, the parent feels the tug of loved ones. Unlike the other groups requesting your time and attention, family members don't write ego-boosting letters or offer to pay your expenses. They seek your presence for who you are—not what you can do for them.[5] Although most of us, when asked to list our priorities, would place the family high on the list, the actual expenditures of our time and energy are often heavily weighted toward the "outside world." It is frequently noted that those on their deathbeds don't say they wish they had spent more time at the office or that they had served on another committee. The regret most often expressed by the person is not having spent more time with his or her family.

Children and teenagers need to feel that they have a place in the world. They need to be secure in their sense of belonging to a family where their presence and their thoughts matter. They need to be able to share their worries, their hopes, and their dreams with respected role models and mentors. If our youth don't have these needs met at home, they will seek other avenues for fulfillment—sometimes with their peers, and in extreme cases, with gangs or other groups with negative agendas. The frightening ability of such organizations to alter and shape attitudes and values of their young "recruits" is just one of many reasons to make the family a center of positive relationships and positive interactions. The family is the major institution for socializing the young, and if it fails, other influences will fill the vacuum.

Because the family has the best and earliest opportunity to affect children's attitudes and moral standards, the value of family activities—for parents and children—cannot be overstated. One father grasped this significance and expressed it well: "I think all this emphasis on communication is phony if you aren't taking the time to *do* things with your children. That's when you have your best conversations—when you're doing something together that you both enjoy."[6] These shared activities provide opportunities for parents and children to discuss a wide range of topics and to build mutual understanding and respect. However, any effort to engage in meaningful conversation with children begins with a good relationship, and good relationships require time.

My oldest brother, J.R., told me that his most cherished memory of our father was a trip that the two of them took when J.R. was a teenager. Our dad was a long-distance truck driver then, and his time spent with the family was limited. He would leave on Monday morning and not return until Friday evening. Therefore, it was a special treat—although one that involved helping with deliveries along the way—to have a whole week alone with his father. The two of them "talked about everything" and got to know each other on a level that they had never before experienced. From that trip, each developed a deeper love and respect for the other. Being treated as an adult instead of the teenager that he was provided a special memory that my brother would value for the rest of his life.

Time and circumstances don't allow all parents to spend a whole week alone with each of their children, but they can find ways to involve family members in activities which might seem ordinary at the moment but are later viewed as special and memorable bits of family history. Whether the parent-child activity involves a daughter's "date" with her father, a father-son athletic outing, a pick-up game of basketball, a mother-daughter shopping excursion, a family picnic in the park, cookies and milk after school, a Sunday afternoon trip for ice cream, or badminton in the backyard, the important issue is the act of being together and sharing time as a family. Even household chores or yard work—when approached with a proper attitude—can provide opportunities to build those special bonds. Working together as equals breaks down barriers that sometimes inhibit free and honest conversation between generations. In such situations, both parents and children—especially teenagers—find it easier to be open and to share thoughts and concerns.

In *Raising Good Children*, Thomas Lickona gives the following account by a father who experienced first-hand some unexpected benefits as he and his son moved a compost pile:

> Sandy was thirteen, and the new school year had gotten off to a pretty rocky start. Problems with peers, insecurity about his place in the group, that sort of thing. As we shoveled dirt and sod that afternoon, we had one of the best conversations we'd had in a long time. We talked about a lot of things: his teachers and how he felt about them, some kids at school who were giving him a hard time, a girl he used to like and a new one he thought he might like, and a discussion of drugs they had in health class. I felt close to him at the end of that day.[7]

In a recent article in *USA Weekend*, families from across America offered their tips for building strong families. Recognizing that the cost of family vacations can be prohibitive, one family, the Paeths from Vancouver, Washington, offered this advice: "Give memories, not things." This simple statement says a lot about family relationships and family ties in general. However, the Paeths apply it specifically by saving all the money that they would otherwise spend throughout the year on individual birthday presents and Christmas gifts and plan one large outing for the whole family that fits their budget.[8] Presumably, all family members would have some input into what that outing would be. The anticipation of the event, as well as the outing itself, would offer opportunities for considerable family conversation, as well as for the peaceful resolution of conflicts or differences of opinion.

Another suggestion for building strong families came from Kay Martin, of Greenville, S.C., who proposed that parents invest fifteen minutes with each child individually every night. From the time her children were infants through their high school years, Mrs. Martin would sit on the side of each child's bed for a few minutes every evening, taking time to share "all kinds of trivia, triumphs, or worries." Today, her grown offspring are carrying on this same family tradition with their own children.[9] Obviously, this family activity involves very little time and no cost. Yet, its value to those involved is priceless.

Wayne Dosdick, author of *The Golden Rules: The Ten Ethical Values Parents Need to Teach Their Children,* supports the Martin family's practice. He advises parents to tuck their children into bed as often as possible "when they are little—and for as long as they will let you."

"When the sun sets and night comes," Rabbi Dosdick says, "your children's fondest hopes, deepest thoughts, most troubling questions and worst fears all come bubbling up to the surface of their consciousness. . . .When you make time to tuck your children into bed, you are there to listen and to talk. You can hear their stories and tell them yours. You can help mold their ideas and beliefs and shape their feelings." These short, but important, shared moments allow parents to enfold their children "in security and love."[10]

Activities involving grandparents and other relatives can also be very meaningful in a child's character development. In his best-selling book, *The 7 Habits of Highly Effective People,* Stephen Covey says that ongoing contact with the extended family—children, parents, grandparents, aunts, uncles, and cousins—"can be a powerful force in helping people have a sense of who they are and where they came from and what they stand for."[11] Especially in this era when families are spread across the nation and around the world, it is good for children to be able to identify with "the tribe," and to know that many people know them and care about them.[12]

Grandparents can also play critical roles in the actual molding and shaping of children's character. They are often willing to spend unhurried hours talking to, playing with, or teaching skills to their grandchildren. In "Letter from A Third-Grader," one child gave her perception of grandparents:

> A grandmother is a lady who has no children of her own. She likes other people's little girls and boys. A grandfather is a man grandmother. He goes for walks with the boys, and they talk about fishing and things like that. . . . When they read to us they don't skip or mind if it's the same story over again. . . . Everybody should try to have a grandmother . . . because they are the only grown-ups who have time.[13]

Even when families can't be physically together, telephone or e-mail communications help to strengthen family ties. Also, the family photo album can assist in building a sense of "belonging, bonding, and continuity."[14] Looking through pictures of the older generation can be an enjoyable and meaningful family activity. Children are intrigued by pictures of parents and grandparents "when they were young." Somehow, they seem to assume that members of the older generation have always been "old." It is a revelation for them to see Mom or Dad as a child or teenager. Time spent together talking about, and often laughing at, old family pictures serves as a kind of personal history lesson, and it also provides an opportunity to put family struggles and triumphs into a moral context.

Playing together is one of the easiest and best ways to build a sense of family unity. This suggestion seems so obvious, but in today's hectic world, we sometimes lose sight of the physical and emotional value of play and relaxation. Whether the play involves board games, softball, or swimming, there will be many opportunities to teach sportsmanship and to develop good character. Perhaps more important, by playing with your children—by enjoying your children—you will show them "that play and laughter are integral parts of life for everyone—regardless of age or place." At the same time, you will be teaching them the importance of keeping "their lives in balance and their perspectives straight."[15]

Wayne Dosdick says that every word that parents and their children speak, every action that parents and their children take, and every deed that parents and their children perform help to create the children's "memory bank." In other words, everything the family does makes a deposit into the memory bank which becomes your children's "permanent record." That record—that memory bank—becomes the parent's history and posterity. For the children, it is their inheritance and their destiny."[16]

Sylvestre Sorola, a wildlife biologist from Texas, was a contributor to the book *More Reflections on the Meaning of Life*. His account of a shared experience with his son seems to provide an appropriate summary of this chapter on family activities. Sorola and his son were together on a hunting trip late in the season. The temperature dropped to ten degrees. The Sorolas could have spent the night in a heated trailer with other hunters, but the son said, "No, Dad. Let's stay in the tent."

The elder Sorola said that they almost froze, but it turned into a truly meaningful event. During the night, the son got up, unzipped the tent, and stepped outside. After a moment, he said, "Dad, Dad. Get up. You've got to see this. It's beautiful. I can see all the stars." Although the father knew exactly what to expect as he stuck his head outside of the tent, he was moved by the majesty of the moment. He said, "The stars were extremely bright, and it looked like they had come down to be a little bit closer to us. It was absolutely beautiful."

Sorola summarized the experience as follows: "That, to me, was life. That happiness that night was what life is all about." Then he added, "Money could not have bought me what we felt. We were together in sort of a hardship situation, even though we had asked for it. There was beauty. There was companionship. There was wonder in his voice."[17]

[1] Unknown Author, *Love Adds a Little Chocolate*, Medard Laz, ed. (Ann Arbor, MI: Servant Publications, 1997), p. 20.

[2] Don E. Eberly, "Building the Habitat of Character," in *The Content of America's Character*, Don Eberly, ed. (Lanham, MD: Madison Books, 1995), p.36.

[3] Max Lucado, *In the Eye of the Storm* (Dallas: Word Publishing, 1991), p. 96.

[4] Ibid., p. 97.

[5] Ibid.

[6] Thomas Lickona, *Raising Good Children* (New York: Bantam Books, 1994), p. 252.

[7] Ibid., p. 254.

[8] "Tips for Strong Families," *USA Weekend*, November 28-30, 1997, p. 11.

[9] Ibid.

[10] Wayne Dosdick, *Golden Rules: The Ten Ethical Values Parents Need to Teach Their Children* (San Francisco: Harper Collins Publishers, 1995), p. 163.

[11] Stephen Covey, *The 7 Habits of Highly Effective People* (New York: Simon & Schuster, 1989), p. 315.

[12] Ibid.

[13] Letter from a Third-Grader, "What's a Grandmother?" *Stories for the Heart*, compiled by Alice Gray (Sisters, OR: Questar Publishers, Inc., 1996), p. 160.

[14] "Tips for Strong Families," op. cit.

[15] Dosdick, op. cit., p. 164.

[16] Ibid., p. 199.

[17] Friend, David and editors of *Life*, *More Reflections on the Meaning of Life* (Boston: Little, Brown, and Company, 1992), p. 54.

Worship together as a family.

The year was 1960. The place was New Orleans. Robert Coles, a young psychiatrist, was rushing to a professional conference when he came upon a nasty mob scene. A crowd of angry protesters—all white—lined the sidewalk, and they were screaming and swearing. There seemed to be no direct target for their anger, but then the marshals drove up to escort a six-year-old girl. She was black, and her name was Ruby Bridges.

When Ruby emerged from the car, the mob's anger intensified. They heckled her, cursed her, and threatened her. Why? They were objecting to the first instance of school desegregation in Louisiana. Day after day the scene was repeated, and Dr. Coles wondered how the circumstances were affecting Ruby and what was going on in her mind. Later, he would have an opportunity to get to know Ruby and to develop an intense respect for her moral character. Over the next several months, he met with her in her home, and from her drawings, he knew that she was aware of her own jeopardy and vulnerability when confronting the mob.

One day Ruby's teacher told Dr. Coles that instead of just walking past the mob as she usually did, Ruby had stopped that morning and had apparently said something to them, thereby arousing their anger even further. Dr. Coles, who by then was seeing Ruby regularly, said, "Ruby, that mob really became quite threatening, and apparently you spoke to them." Ruby calmly denied having talked to the mob of protesters.

Trying a different tack, Dr. Coles then asked, "Ruby, what was going on? The teacher said she saw you talking. She looked out the window, and your lips were moving at a pretty fast clip there for a while." Seated at the kitchen table in her home, Ruby replied, "Well, I was not talking to that crowd of people." Probing further, as psychiatrists are trained to do, Dr. Coles asked, "Well then, Ruby, who were you talking to?" At that point, Ruby looked straight at Dr. Coles and said, "I was talking to God. Because I saw those people, and they reminded me of the prayer."

Somewhat surprised by her answer, the psychiatrist continued with his questions, asking Ruby what she meant about "the prayer." The little girl said, "I prayed for them." Dr. Coles, again amazed at her response, said, "Why would you want to pray for those people? They were the people who were heckling you and frightening you." With serenity and dignity beyond her years, the child posed a question herself: "Well, don't you think they need praying for?"

"Ruby," Dr. Coles asked, "What do you say in those prayers?" Ruby replied, "Please, God, try to forgive these people, 'cause they don't know what they are doing." At that point, Dr. Coles says, "I wasn't so quick then with any more questions. I was silenced."[1]

Even adults with the highest levels of character development and integrity would be challenged in the face of such undeserved hostility. Most would be tempted to lash out and respond in kind, and it would be easy to hate the perpetrators of these personal attacks. How, then, could a six-year-old child demonstrate such charity and courage? Dr. Coles found the answer as he became more familiar with Ruby and her family. "It became apparent," he said, "that she was receiving the support and guidance of her church, of her community—and most important of all—the support of her family. The principles of charity, compassion, and forgiveness, that Ruby had learned in her home and in her church had obviously made a profound impression.

Robert Coles was deeply touched by Ruby's moral courage and spiritual perception, as he was by ten-year-old Daniel, who was dying of leukemia. The boy had developed a habit of asking his doctors and nurses if they ever prayed for their patients, including him. He also said that he was praying for them. Taken aback by the child's comments, the hospital personnel asked Dr. Coles to do a psychiatric evaluation of Daniel to see what was "troubling" him.

Because of his own medical training, Dr. Coles initially assumed that Daniel was praying out of desperation, imploring God to allow him to survive the devastating disease that had left him weak and profoundly ill. As he talked with Daniel, however, Dr. Coles realized how important the child's religious faith was to him and how earnestly he was trying to relate it to his life's experiences. Face-to-face with his own mortality, Daniel demonstrated genuine compassion for others and expressed concern for the staff who had to deal with so many sick children. From Daniel, Dr. Coles learned a "lifelong clinical lesson"—that children "very much need a sense of purpose and direction in life, a set of values grounded in moral introspection—a spiritual life that is given sanction by their parents and others in the adult world."[2]

Dr. Coles said that Daniel had taught him a very important lesson. Daniel caused him to see that medical professionals should not leap to the conclusion that a child can't give serious thought to the meaning of life "without being a candidate for a doctor's scrutiny." The child's spirituality led the renowned child psychiatrist and Pulitzer Prize-winning author to appreciate the spirituality of other children and to understand that "we honor our children by taking the moral and spiritual side of their lives seriously."[3]

Most children will not face the moral and spiritual challenges that confronted Ruby and Daniel. However, as they move through childhood and adolescence, their character will be tested repeatedly by temptations such as underage drinking, substance abuse, shoplifting, cheating in school and irresponsible sexual behavior. Adolescents desperately want to fit in and to be part of the crowd. Peer pressure is strong and intense. Only those who have a strong sense of self-esteem, who are comfortable with themselves, and who have a solid moral foundation will have the courage to withstand those temptations and pressures.

Intuitively, we might assume that young people who apply principles of faith in their lives would be less likely to be involved in delinquent behavior—which is, after all, a character issue—than those who do not. It is not surprising, therefore, that formal research supports this assumption. For example, the National Longitudinal Study on Adolescent Health involved more than 12,000 teenagers across America. Researchers found that almost 88 percent of the youths reported that they believed in religion and prayer. When compared with other adolescents in the study, those who placed importance on faith and prayer not only were less likely to use substances such as drugs and alcohol and were less likely to be involved in early sexual activity, but they also had higher levels of self-esteem.[4]

Similar results were reported recently by Bruce Chadwick, director of the Center for Studies of the Family at Brigham Young University. Over the past thirty years, he and his colleagues have polled thousands of teenagers. Repeatedly, they have found that adolescents who practice "religious behavior in private, such as reading Scriptures and praying, are less likely to experiment with drugs, have premarital sex, or commit crimes."[5]

Will participating in public and private worship guarantee that children will grow up to be people of good character? Obviously, no single influence can offer such assurance. Many children and youth who have had no exposure to religious instruction exhibit moral strength and courage. However, parents who involve their family in worship services and who—most important—model the principles of goodness, mercy, and honesty in their own lives provide important spiritual nourishment for their children. The children can draw on that strength in times of moral challenge. Their faith will serve as a "bulwark against a culture that preaches a pleasure now, this-is-all-there-is view of life."[6]

It is unfortunate that our society has become so secularized that many religiously faithful adults are reluctant to speak openly of the importance of their religious beliefs and the spiritual principles that undergird and guide their behavior. Many of us, says Robert Coles, "feel troubled by the matter of religion as it connects with our children's life, in school and at home and in the neighborhood, as if it the subject were somehow a threat to this nation's secular society."[7] In our efforts to be "politically correct," we may behave publicly— and even privately at times—as if our faith does not matter to us.[8]

To ignore the value of religious instruction and family worship in the development of good character in children is to ignore a very basic need. After years of studying the moral and spiritual development of children, Robert Coles says that he has come to understand that children "constantly ask their whys" and "seek moral reasons upon which to gird their present and future life."[9] Anyone who has spent time with young children knows that even preschool children are constantly trying to understand the world in which they live. Such questioning continues throughout childhood and intensifies during adolescence, as teenagers ponder their future and their place in the world.

Plato once advised parents to bequeath to their children not riches, but the spirit of reverence. Centuries later, Albert Schweitzer said as he reflected on his early worship experiences, "From the services in which I joined as a child, I have taken with me into life a feeling for what is solemn, and a need for quiet reflection, without which I cannot realize the meaning of my life."[10] In contrast to activities in our society which are often coarse and profane, religious services can help the young to develop an appreciation for the sacred and a reverence for life.

Etiquette expert Letitia Baldridge states in *Complete Guide to the New Manners for the 90s* that parents who take their children to a house of worship regularly "may be giving them the strongest and most effective help and support they will ever have in their lives." She encourages parents to read Bible stories to their children every night, "explaining the moral lessons contained in those pages." This practice, she says will instill in the hearts of children a respect not only for God, but for other human beings as well. Why would this advice be included in a book about etiquette? Mrs. Baldridge explains: "After all, a respect for God and for other human beings [is the] foundation of manners, morals, ethics and values."[11]

In *The 7 Habits of Highly Effective Families*, Stephen Covey says that worshipping together is one of the characteristics of happy and healthy families. When family members worship together, they help to "strengthen one another's faith as well as their own."[12] These shared worship experiences help to strengthen unity and provide a moral foundation for the family. Also, participating in religious sacraments, such as holy communion or the Seder meal, reminds children that they belong not only to their human family, but to a larger family of faith. Reading from the sacred texts or hearing stories about the heroes of the faith provides children with worthy moral models to follow and also gives them a sense of the continuity of life—it gives them a past, a present and a future with meaning.

Marian Wright Edelman, founder and president of the Children's Defense Fund, grew up in South Carolina during the era of segregation. In her book, *The Measure of Our Success*, she explains that it was her early religious experiences that led her into a life of service to others. "Service," she says, "was as essential a part of my upbringing as eating and sleeping and going to school." She adds that the church was "a hub of Black children's social existence, and caring black adults were buffers against the segregated and hostile outside world." Everywhere she went as a child, she was "under the watchful eye of members of the congregation and community," and the adults taught lessons about life and service, not "by sermonizing, but by personal example."[13]

Service to others and to the community, good citizenship, honesty, and personal responsibility are all important aspects of good character. They are also basic to a democratic society. When French political scientist Alexis de Tocqueville visited America in the early nineteenth century, he saw a direct relationship between American religion and American democracy. He noted that "all the things that democracy relies on, religion teaches."[14] Almost two centuries later, we might take Tocqueville's observation a step further and say that all the things that good character relies on, most faiths teach. As just one illustration, every major religion has some version of the Golden Rule—the principle that we should treat others as we wish to be treated. (See Appendix A for variations of the Golden Rule.)

Traditionally, three institutions have shared the responsibility of developing good character in American children and youth: the home; the church, synagogue, or mosque; and the school. Although their roles are different, common sense suggests that the efforts of all three will be more effective if they are mutually reinforcing. By providing direct teaching in virtues such as honesty, compassion, good stewardship, and service to others; by helping children develop their talents through participating in church choirs or pageants; by offering leadership development through youth groups; by exposing children and teenagers to worthy role models; and by helping children and teenagers develop a sense of meaning and purpose in life, religion can play a major role in character development.

Messages from the media and the lifestyles of some current celebrities would lead our youth to believe that the pleasure of the moment is all that matters. Those of us who have lived longer know that there is more to life than that. Many of us also believe that it is easier to confront the really difficult questions of life if we are standing on a firm foundation of faith. As Wayne Dosdick observes, "the world's spiritual traditions—rooted in ancient and eternal wisdom" have much to teach us, about our own character and that of our children. To seek and to share that wisdom is to leave a valuable and lasting legacy to those whose character we are attempting to influence.[15]

[1] Robert Coles, "Listening to Children," Public Television presentation, September 22, 1995. (Videotapes of that program are available from PBS Home Video, 1320 Braddock Place, Alexandria, VA 22314-1698.)

[2] Robert Coles, *The Moral Intelligence of Children*, (New York: Random House, 1997), pp. 175-177.

[3] Ibid., p. 178.

[4] Michael Resnick, et al., "Protecting Adolescents from Harm," *Journal of the American Medical Association*, September 10, 1997, p. 830.

[5] Arvil Stancil, "Time Tests Youth Ministers," Burlington (NC) *Times News*, October 21, 1997.

[6] Thomas Lickona, *Raising Good Children*, (New York: Bantam Books, 1994), p. 329.

[7] Coles, *The Moral Intelligence of Children*, op. cit., p. 178.

[8] Stephen L. Carter, *The Culture of Disbelief: How American Law and Politics Trivialize Religious Devotion* (New York: Anchor Books, 1993).

[9] Coles, *The Moral Intelligence of Children,* op. cit., p. 178.

[10] Charles L. Wallis, ed., *The Treasure Chest* (New York: Harper & Row Publishers, 1965), p. 131.

[11] Letitia Baldridge, *Complete Guide to the New Manners for the 90s* (New York: Rawson Associates, 1990), p. 37.

[12] Stephen Covey, *The 7 Habits of Highly Effective Families,* (New York: Golden Books, 1997), pp. 279, 300.

[13] Marian Wright Edelman, *The Measure of Our Success,* (Boston: Beacon Press, 1992), pp. 3-4.

[14] Jean Beth Elshtain, quoted by Lex Alexander, "Religion Plays Essential Role in Democracy," Greensboro (NC) *News and Record,* November 11, 1996.

[15] Wayne Dosdick, *Golden Rules: The Ten Ethical Values Parents Need to Teach Their Children* (San Francisco: Harper Collins, Publishers, 1995), p. 4.

Don't provide your children access to alcohol or drugs. Model appropriate behavior regarding alcohol and drugs.

An 18-year-old college student recently wrote to "Dear Abby" to express her concern about the extent of the drug and alcohol problem among the youth of today. "Seven years ago when I was eleven," she said, "I, too, wanted to get high once, 'just to see what it was like.' Well, four years and one arrest, a long-term psychiatric hospitalization and $30,000 later, I finally admitted that I had a serious problem—not to mention the pain and grief I caused my family." Looking back on her involvement in substance abuse, she said, "I never intended to become an addict. Nobody does. I just wanted to try it because all the 'cool' people did drugs, and I wanted to be 'cool,' too."[1]

The young woman, who signed her letter "Older, Wiser, and Clean," stated that by the time she was 15, she weighed only 85 pounds and had more cocaine, methamphetamine, alcohol, and marijuana in her blood "than any human body should have been able to tolerate." Three of her former "partying" buddies died of drug-related causes. Having been in recovery for three years and now attending college, she shared her story in the hope that it might cause even one young person to stop and think about the dangers of experimenting with drugs.[2]

"Older, Wiser, and Clean" followed a pattern which is all too familiar to teachers and counselors, and those who work with adolescent substance abusers. Some parents may be shocked at her admission that she started using drugs at the age of 11. Unfortunately, many young people first begin to use drugs in the very early stages of adolescence, with some beginning to drink alcohol or use tobacco products as early as age 9 or 10. The most typical progression for young teens is from the *illicit* use of *legal* substances (tobacco, inhalants, and alcohol) to the use of *illegal* drugs, such as marijuana and other drugs.[3] Not all youth who smoke will use marijuana, nor will all who drink alcohol go on to use other drugs. However, an adolescent who has used tobacco or alcohol, is 65 times more likely to move on to marijuana than a non-smoker/non-drinker. Teens who have smoked marijuana at least once are 104 times more likely to advance to using cocaine than those who have never smoked marijuana.[4]

Consider the following accounts of recovering addicts from *Real People Tell Their Stories*, a publication of the Center for Substance Abuse Treatment:

> I started drinking way back in the sixth grade. I would get a beer for my parents out of the refrigerator, then I began to drink myself, sometimes before breakfast or even on my way to school. It was the safest drug to start with. Then I went on to pot and cocaine.
>
> Terry, Bradenton, Florida

> I started drinking when I was 14, and as things progressed in my life, I used pot, acid, speed, cocaine, whatever I could get.
>
> Gloria, Bronx, New York

> I began using when I was 12. . . . I started with alcohol and marijuana and, of course, that led to harder drugs in no time. . . . I thought I could always stop at any time if necessary.
>
> Joy, Des Moines, Iowa[5]

In my work as a counselor and later as a supervisor of school counselors, social workers, and psychologists, I have known personally and heard about young people who developed a chemical dependency at a very early age. Amazingly, many of these children and early adolescents were able to hide their drinking or use of other drugs from their parents. One mother, upon hearing that her well-liked, honor-roll son had a serious drinking problem, was stunned. "I didn't know. I didn't know," she said sadly. "He came and kissed me good night every time he came home. I never smelled anything. I never had reason to suspect that he was drinking." Her son, who seemed relieved that his "secret" was finally out, confessed that he had been drinking on a daily basis for several years and simply used mouthwash to conceal the smell of the alcohol. In a similar vein, a college undergraduate told her instructor, "I knew a lot of kids who did drugs all the time, and their parents didn't have a clue."[6]

To say that substance abuse is a threat to the future of our youth is an understatement. Parents, law enforcement officers, counselors, and teachers witness first-hand the toll that alcohol and drugs take on the attitudes, behavior, moral judgment, and physical health of adolescents. The problem has taken on epidemic proportions, and child psychiatrist Mitchell Rosenthal is not alone in his belief that "youthful alcohol/drug abuse today is society's single most terrifying problem."[7] William Damon, who works with parents around the country in addressing problems of youth, describes the drug problem as "our society's most cancerous problem, spreading rapidly wherever it takes root and decimating the lives of those that it affects."[8]

During the 1980s, there was a significant public relations effort to educate Americans about the dangers of substance abuse. Public service announcements promoted the notion that using drugs was neither smart nor healthy. Kids were urged to "just say no." Those efforts have lost momentum in recent years, however, and culture has made the use of drugs and alcohol more attractive to our youth. Interestingly, Americans consistently identify drug use as one of the top problems in our schools. Yet, many don't seem to recognize the extent of the risk to their own children, their own schools, and their own communities.[9] Some research studies suggest that "drug use among children is 10 times more prevalent than parents suspect."[10] To illustrate, a 1998 study by the Partnership for a Drug-Free America revealed that Baby Boomer parents typically underestimated "the availability of marijuana, their children's view of its risks, and whether their children's friends were smoking."[11]

What do current statistics tell us about drug usage among our young? I will not attempt to address all types of drugs, but I believe it is critically important for parents to be aware of the "gateway drugs" and their effects. These are tobacco products, alcohol, and marijuana, whose use often leads to more serious drug use.

First, let's look at tobacco. Despite compelling evidence that cigarette smoking causes lung cancer and using smokeless tobacco (chewing tobacco and snuff) causes cancer of the mouth and throat, 43 percent of American high school students smoke or chew tobacco, and the number is rising.[12] In addition to the threats to their physical health, youth who smoke are also at much greater risk for all other drug use.[13]

Marijuana is the illegal drug most commonly used in America. It is a gateway drug because very few adolescents move on to using other illegal drugs without first using marijuana. Research indicates that almost 40 percent of teenagers try marijuana before they graduate from high school and that the number of 12- to 17-year-olds using marijuana doubled between 1992 and 1996.[14] Yet, some parents—especially those who experimented with drugs in their own youth—tend to minimize the dangers of using marijuana. What many adults don't realize is that the marijuana produced today is from 5 to 20 times more potent than that which was available as recently as 15 years ago[15] and that use of the drug begins at a much earlier age today. The average age of first use of marijuana now is 13.5.[16] In the 1960s, students beginning to experiment with marijuana were typically of college age. Today, they are in middle school!

The third gateway drug is alcohol—the number-one drug problem among the young. Because of social acceptance of drinking, easy access to alcohol, and extensive promotion of alcoholic beverages in our society, it is not surprising that alcohol is the most widely used and abused drug. So widespread is its use that research studies show that almost 90 percent of American youth have tried alcoholic beverages by their senior year in high school. Even though the legal drinking age is 21, students of junior and senior high school age drink 35 percent of all the wine coolers sold in America.[17]

Because of the availability of alcohol in numerous homes, many children and youth start drinking in their own home or that of a friend. Although it is illegal, some parents even give alcohol to their teenagers, rationalizing that they want them to learn to "drink responsibly." When they do this, parents are unwittingly telling their children that adults condone their doing things that are illegal—as long as they do them "responsibly."[18]

Drinking is a particular hazard to children and early teenagers. In addition to the other more obvious risks, the use of alcohol at an early age dramatically increases the chance that the person will become an alcoholic. A study by the National Institutes of Health involving face-to-face interviews with almost 43,000 people showed that youths who begin drinking at or before the age of 14 are *four times* as likely to develop a lifetime dependency on alcohol than are those who wait until at least age 20 before starting to drink alcohol.[19] The study also revealed that those who began drinking before the age of 13 and who had a family history of alcoholism had a *60 percent* chance of becoming an alcoholic.[20] Sadly, more than one-fifth of all of the clients admitted to alcohol or other drug-treatment programs in the United States in 1995 were under age 24, with almost 7 percent being under age 15.[21]

Substance abuse among the young takes a heavy toll on the individual, the family and larger society. A direct result of youthful drinking is the very high incidence of alcohol-related accidents, which are the leading cause of death for those between the ages of 15 and 24. (The National Highway Traffic Safety Commission reports that more than 60 percent of adolescents involved in automobile accidents have been drinking.[22]) The combination of chemical impairment, youthful risk-taking, and limited driving experience is deadly. Few communities have escaped the pain of seeing the lives of bright, promising young people end tragically amid broken glass, beer cans, and crumpled steel.

Not only do alcohol and drugs impair coordination and judgment, but they also break down moral inhibitions, causing kids to lose self-control and do things that they would not even consider doing if they were sober. For example, some studies show that as many as 95 percent of teenage pregnancies occur when at least one of the partners is under the influence of intoxicants.[23] The use of alcohol at an early age is also associated with sexually transmitted diseases, other drug usage, suicide, and depression.[24] All of these effects threaten the future health and safety of our young.

Sometimes, the statistics almost overwhelm us. Is there anything we can do to stem the awful tide of substance abuse? The problem is so widespread that some parents feel helpless, but it is important to understand that you *can* make a difference for your own children. While there are no guarantees that your children will remain free of drugs and alcohol, you can increase the odds that they will develop the strength of character to make responsible decisions.

Despite peer pressure, the anxieties of adolescence, a youthful desire for "sophistication," and media messages that glamorize the use of drugs and alcohol, the family is *the* most powerful influence on whether a young person will become a substance abuser. Alan Leshner, of the National Institute on Drug Abuse says that "twenty years of scientific research have shown that direct parental involvement in the life of the child is the most protective factor in increasing the odds that a kid will remain drug-free."[25] Similarly, Robert DuPont states in *Getting Tough on Gateway Drugs* that "an educated and committed family is the nation's best defense against drug and alcohol problems."[26]

The first and most important step parents can take is to be sure that they *do not provide access to drugs or alcohol* to their children. I have recently heard about several situations in which parents reportedly used drugs in the presence of their children—and some even smoked marijuana with their own teenagers. Most parents wouldn't consider providing marijuana or other illegal drugs to their children, but what about alcohol? A recent study on adolescent health revealed that alcohol was readily available in over one-fourth (28.5 percent) of the thousands of homes surveyed.[27]

In some communities, parents even provide kegs of beer for their teenagers' parties. Others provide easy access to their own supplies of alcohol. One mother spoke a painful truth when she said: "Parents often permit what should not be tolerated. We act as if we think it's funny when punch gets spiked or when Coke bottles are filled with liquor. We are against drinking, yet we give silent approval to it."[28] Not surprisingly, school-aged children who are allowed to drink alcohol at home are more likely to use alcohol and other drugs outside the home.[29]

It's also important for you, as a parent, to be well informed about drugs and alcohol, to educate your children about the dangers of substance abuse, and to take a strong stand concerning your own beliefs. Children are especially vulnerable to peer pressure and to the threats of substance abuse at the transition periods—times when they move from one developmental stage to another. Obviously, the first big transition is from the security of home and family to school. There children encounter behavior and attitudes that may differ from—and even challenge—what their parents have tried to teach them. Another particularly critical transition occurs when children advance from elementary school to middle school or junior high. It is at this time that a child is likely to be exposed to drug use for the first time. Other transitions are from middle or junior high school to high school and from high school to college, where both the opportunities and the temptations to use drugs and alcohol are even greater than before. At each of these periods, parents need to be especially careful to maintain open, frank, and mutually respectful communication with their children.[30]

It is never too early to begin talking with your children about drugs. The natural curiosity of young children provides many opportunities for discussion and for teaching children to make good decisions. I have a friend who really focused on the impact that every decision can have on a child's character and conduct, and his strategy certainly applies to the use of drugs and alcohol. As his sons were growing up, he told them to think about what they wanted to do in the future and what kind of person they wanted to be. He taught them to move toward their goal, *one day at a time* and *one decision at a time.* "If you will evaluate every decision on the basis of whether or not it will help you reach that goal," he told them, "you will stay out of trouble, and each of those decisions will help to build your character. If you reach your goal, it will be your character that takes you there." The expression "one by one" became a family code for doing the right thing. To this day, he and his now-grown sons end their telephone conversations with the words "one by one," and they sign their father-son electronic mail with the symbol 1/1.

It's important to talk openly and directly about your beliefs concerning drugs and alcohol. Some parents seem to avoid the subject, as if their ignoring it might make the problem go away. Others simply assume that their children will absorb their parents' values. The risks are too great to leave such an important matter to chance; nor can we afford to let our silence imply approval of substance abuse. The Partnership for a Drug-Free America recently released a report indicating that children and adolescents who learn about the risks of drugs at home are significantly less likely to use drugs than those whose parents avoid the subject. Also, among 9- to 12-year-olds, the number-one reason children gave for not using drugs was that their parents would be upset.[31]

Similarly, studies by the Johnson Institute and the Hazelden Center also confirm that the single most influential factor in a child's decision not to use drugs is the child's "understanding of the degree of parental upset if s/he is caught using." (These studies also revealed that youth who have a religious affiliation with, and participate in the activities of a church, synagogue, or mosque are less likely to use drugs or alcohol.) [32]

In addition to making their position on drugs and alcohol clear, parents also need to establish and enforce standards for their children's behavior. It is natural for children—especially adolescents—to challenge rules and to seek freedoms before they are ready for them. However, for their own protection they need—and most want—limits and controls. The following excerpt from a keynote address on "Drugs and the American Family" by Dr. Mitchell Rosenthal makes a strong case for setting and enforcing limits:

Nothing today is as important for parents to recognize as the need to set limits. Parents have got to be able to take positions about bedtime or drinking or sleepovers. They've got to know where they stand on curfews, school-night dating, chaperones or study time—and they've got to hold that line in the face of bickering and blackmail and all the other tactics youngsters use to get their way. And the payout is that children who are IN control because they are UNDER control feel better about themselves—and feel better about their parents.[33]

Where drugs and alcohol are concerned, it is critically important to communicate clearly and unequivocally a no-use message. Simply stated, let your children know that there is to be *no alcohol* and *no drug use* at any time, whether in your home, a friend's home, or anywhere else. Let your children know what the rules are and the consequences for breaking them. As an example, consider the parents of Mark and Donna Allenbach, who clearly understood this principle. When the Allenbach children were approaching the age to receive a driver's license, their father told them, "If either of you ever drink and drive, you can say good-bye to anything to do with our cars. There will be no second chances. Once, and it's over. You are too important to lose."[34]

It's also helpful to rehearse with your children what they should say or do when someone offers them drugs or alcohol or pressures them to do something that conflicts with their family's value system. This will enable them to plan in advance what they will say in an actual situation at a party, at school, or at the mall. Just as fire drills help to save lives in times of real emergencies, these "decision drills" can save your children from some potentially life-threatening situations.

The single most powerful weapon that parents have in the war against drugs is their own personal example. With alcohol and drugs, as with other issues of character, actions speak louder than words. Parents who walk in the door every evening and mix a drink or light a cigarette whenever they feel tense are communicating a strong message about drug use and about how to cope with life's problems.

Those who make alcohol the centerpiece of their parties teach their children that you can't expect to have a good time without drinking. At a minimum, a "do as I say and not as I do" attitude confuses children and youth, and it erodes their confidence in their parents.[35]

With drugs, as with other issues of character, the lessons learned at home are the ones that affect a child the most. Most school alcohol and substance-abuse programs and public services messages tell youths to avoid using drugs because it's not smart to do so. Such efforts miss the point that decisions about drugs and alcohol are more than intellectual questions and they are more than matters of temperance. Ultimately, they are moral issues—issues of character.

People of good character learn to control their impulses, and they avoid doing things that hurt or harm themselves or others. As parents and educators, our challenge is to help children and youth to understand what drugs and alcohol can do to their will, their self-control, their judgment and their behavior, and to equip them with the strength of character to avoid the pitfalls of substance abuse. By our words and our deeds, we should all strive to guide them toward future success, *one day at a time* and *one decision at a time.*

. . . .

[1] Abigail Van Buren, "Dear Abby," Burlington (NC) *Times News,* April 10, 1998.

[2] Ibid.

[3] *Preventing Drug Abuse Among Children and Adolescents,* National Institute on Drug Abuse, National Institutes of Health Publication No. 97-4212.

[4] Ibid., p. 7.

[5] *Real People Tell Their Stories,* Center for Substance Abuse Treatment, Substance Abuse and Mental Health Services Administration, U. S. Department of Health and Human Services (undated).

[6] Thomas Lickona, *Raising Good Children* (New York: Bantam Books, 1994), p. 376.

[7] *As Parents, We Will . . A Guide for Parents,* (Grosse Pointe Farms, MI: Substance Abuse Community Council of Grosse Pointe, 1994), p. 5.

[8] William Damon, *The Youth Charter: How Communities Can Work Together to Raise Standards for All Our Children* (New York: The Free Press, 1997), p. 128.

[9] *Schools Without Drugs: What Works* (Washington: U. S. Department of Education, 1992), p. 2.

[10] Ibid.

[11] Larry McShane, "Parents Clueless about Drugs," Burlington (NC) *Times News*, April 13, 1998.

[12] Lauran Neergaard, "Study: Teen Tobacco Use at 43 Percent and Rising," Burlington (NC) *Times News*, April 3, 1998.

[13] *Growing up Drug-Free: A Parent's Guide to Prevention* (Washington, DC: U. S. Department of Education, undated), p. 3.

[14] Joyce Kraweic, "Teens Using More Drugs," Greensboro (NC) *News and Record*, September 1, 1996.

[15] *Schools without Drugs: What Works*, op. cit.

[16] *Marijuana: Facts Parents Need to Know*, National Institute on Drug Abuse, U. S. Department of Health and Human Services, NIH Publication No. 9504036, 1995.

[17] *Schools Without Drugs: What Works*, op. cit., p. 8.

[18] *As Parents, We Will . . . .*, op. cit., p. 31l.

[19] Bridget F. Grant and Deborah A. Dawson, "Age at Onset of Alcohol Use and Its Association with DSM-IV Alcohol Abuse and Dependence," *Journal of Substance Abuse*, Vol. 9, 1997, pp. 103-110.

[20] Sally Squires, "Early Drinking Puts Kids at Risk for Alcoholism," *Washington Post*, Reprinted in Greensboro (NC) *News and Record*, March 23, 1998.

[21] *NCADD Fact Sheet: Youth, Alcohol, and Other Drugs*, (New York: National Council on Alcoholism and Drug Dependence, Inc.), February, 1998.

[22] *As Parents, We Will . . .* , op. cit., p. 8.

[23] Ibid.

[24] Bridget F. Grant and Deborah A. Dawson, op. cit., pp. 103-104.

[25] Per Ola and Emilly D'Aulaire, "How to Raise Drug-Free Kids," *Reader's Digest*, April, 1997, pp. 151-160.

[26] *As Parents, We Will . . .*, op. cit., p. 28.

[27] Michael Resnick et al., "Protecting Adolescents from Harm," *Journal of the American Medical Association*, September 10, 1997, p. 823.

[28] Haim Ginott, *Between Parent and Teenager* (New York: The Macmillan Company, 1969), p.186.

[29] *As Parents, We Will . . .* op. cit., p. 21.

[30] *Preventing Drug Abuse Among Children and Adolescents*, op. cit., p. 6.

[31] "The Boomer-Rang: Baby-Boomers Seriously Underestimating Presence of Drugs in Their Children's Lives," Press Release of the Partnership for a Drug-Free America, April 13, 1998.

[32] *As Parents, We Will . . .* op. cit., p.21.

[33] Ibid., p. 5.

[34] Ola Per and Emily D'Aulaire, op. cit., p. 157.

[35] Thomas Knowles and W. R. Spence, *Parenting Teens: Straight Talk* (Waco, Texas: WRS Group, 1993, p. 8.

Plan family service projects or civic activities.

Recently I've had the opportunity to serve on several scholarship committees, and it has been most encouraging to interact with bright high school seniors who genuinely want to make a difference in the world. Although they are only seventeen or eighteen years old, most of them have already amassed an impressive record of service to others—in a school system in which community service is *not* a graduation requirement. They are involved as volunteers at the homeless shelter, the family abuse center, Habitat for Humanity, the Civil Air Patrol, and at local hospitals and homes for the aged.

One young woman helps to host dances for mentally handicapped adults; she also provides ice water and pleasant conversation to the residents of a rest home in her community. Another teenager (who works part-time, in addition to maintaining honor-roll status in a demanding academic load) gives up one night every week to read to children at the shelter for abused families. Several of the candidates have participated in service trips with their church youth groups, rebuilding homes in Appalachia or working with children in underdeveloped countries. When asked what they have learned from their service activities, their statements are very similar:

"I got more out of it than the people we were there to help."

"I learned to appreciate people who are different from me."

"I found out how satisfying it is to help others."

These teenagers from my community are like countless other youth across America who have learned to show their love and compassion for others through community service. Consider for example, the difference that an adolescent made for an elderly man in a rest home in Texas. The man, Mr. Morgan, was old, crippled, and apparently forgotten by family and former friends. He spent his days just waiting to die, and his only regular visitor was a pastor who continued to drop by, although he had given up trying to cheer the sad, lonely old man. One day, however, the pastor found Mr. Morgan sitting up, smiling and eager to talk. What made the dramatic difference? Mr. Morgan had received a letter that morning—the first he had received in *twelve years*!

The writer of the letter was Nancy, a thirteen-year-old who has taken on a personal mission of writing to lonely people. She collects from churches and rest homes the names of elderly people who don't have relatives or friends, and she sends them happy, humorous accounts of her family and her school. One wealthy seventy-eight-year-old recipient of Nancy's letters had lived in aloof isolation for more than fifteen years. Suddenly, she too changed and became friendlier and more pleasant to be with. Why did this happen? She explains it this way: "The day I saw Nancy's letter in the mailbox and realized the postman had not made a mistake was the day I admitted to myself just how sour and shriveled my life had become. If someone Nancy's age thinks I'm worth writing to, well I guess it's not too late to start living again."[1]

Another teenager who contradicts the image of youth as troubled and self-centered is Adam Chestnut, who lives in Toronto, Ohio. Alan heard about national Make a Difference Day, which is celebrated in October of each year. Wanting to make a difference himself, Alan wrote a note to each person on his paper route, asking them to donate used clothes and household items to Goodwill Industries. The fourteen-year-old assumed responsibility for collecting and delivering the donations. On October 25, 1997, Alan—

with the help of his mother, who drove the family truck—collected fifty bags of donated goods and carried them to Goodwill. For his efforts, Alan received a National Make a Difference Day award of $2,000—which he donated to Goodwill Industries. Why did he do all of that hard work? Alan said that delivering the items to Goodwill gave him one of the greatest feelings he had ever felt. "When you help somebody out," he said, "that's helping you out, too. It lifts your spirits to see people's faces. You can see the happiness."[2]

All of these young people have learned some lasting lessons about caring and giving and serving. Where did they learn those lessons? I don't know their parents, but it would probably be safe to assume that much of the teaching occurred in the home. Parents who expect their children to show concern and compassion for others, who teach their children the importance of participating in service to the community, and who model service and good citizenship in their own lives are making important investments in the future of their children, their community, and their country. Both common sense and research confirm that those who involve themselves in helping others are happier and healthier than those who think only of their own comfort and convenience. There is an enduring truth in Albert Schweitzer's observation: "I don't know what your destiny will be, but one thing I do know: the only ones among you who will be truly happy are those who have sought and found how to serve."

In past generations, children in this country were often expected to look after younger siblings, help in the fields, prepare meals, or assist in caring for elderly or sick relatives. They had serious responsibilities, true, but they also had the benefits of feeling that they were making real contributions to their family life. By contrast, many of today's youth are totally dependent on their parents, and they contribute little or nothing to the functioning of the family. Because they have everything given to them, it is not surprising that some children and youth are self-centered and lack focus. Despite having so many material things and so little responsibility, some are bored and restless and have low levels of self-esteem.

Involvement in meaningful service to others can counteract these negative feelings by giving children and youth a sense of purpose and a feeling of being needed. At the same time, their character—their ability to look beyond their own desires—will be strengthened. In *Principle-Centered Leadership*, Stephen Covey states that "the philosophy that we will find our life when we lose it in service is a totally true paradox." He adds, "If our intent is to serve, to bless others, without self-concern, a by-product of service comes within —a kind of psychological, emotional, spiritual reward in the form of internal security and peace."[3]

Many teachers and counselors have witnessed first-hand the difference that service projects can have on the behavior and attitudes of children. For example, I heard recently about a low-achieving middle school child who was selected to read to kindergarten children on a regular basis. Not only did he help the five-year-olds, but his own confidence and scholastic performance improved. Often, children who are at risk of dropping out of school or who have behavior problems experience a complete turnaround when they are given helping roles in the school or community. Research confirms that youth who have opportunities to care for others through community service have higher levels of self-esteem, less depression, better school attendance, and a greater sense of social responsibility.[4]

Helping children and youth discover the meaning and joy of serving others is one of the most important tasks of parenthood. It is also a critical component of the development of good character. In "The Guiding Conscience," Stephen Covey states that "the most significant work we ever do, in our whole world, in our whole life, is done within the four walls of our own home." He adds that "all mothers and fathers, whatever their stations in life, can make the most significant of contributions by imprinting the spirit of service on the souls of their children, so that the children grow up committed to making a difference."[5]

At the heart of service—and good character—is a sense of caring and concern for others. Parents' overt teaching about the importance of being compassionate and their personal examples of service can help to teach children to care. However, to make an indelible impression, parents need to actively involve their children in service projects. They need to apply the ancient Chinese proverb which advises: *Tell me, I forget. Show me, I remember. Involve me, I understand.* Simply stated, children learn to care by engaging in acts of caring and service. Through these acts, they develop empathy, a sense of purpose and a commitment to something beyond themselves.

Psychologist John Rosemond believes that one of the best ways to begin teaching children about service to others is for the family to mirror the expectations that society expects of its citizens. The same values that hold the society together—respect for others, responsibility, honesty, etc.—should be family values as well. By involving children in volunteer projects, parents help their children learn "that service—not self-interest—holds our world together."[6] Thomas Lickona supports Dr. Rosemond's position. He says that "if more children learned early in life that they have responsibilities as well as rights, there'd be fewer teenagers, and fewer adults, who are always demanding their rights but have no sense of their obligations."[7]

There are numerous opportunities for family service projects in every community. Such projects don't have to be elaborate or expensive, and even young children can participate. Simple acts such as carrying food to a neighbor who is ill, mowing an elderly person's lawn, donating outgrown clothing and toys to charity, shopping for someone who is disabled, baby-sitting without charge for a family in crisis, or participating in a school beautification project can help young people learn the joys of helping others and develop habits of service. Simultaneously, family ties are strengthened as parents and children work together in service to the larger community. Together, they experience the unique joy and satisfaction that come only from helping others.

Barry and Linda Appelget, of Greensboro, North Carolina, provide an excellent example of how to teach the value of service. The Applegets wanted their children to understand that there was more to their community than the pleasant neighborhood where they lived. When the children were very young, the family began working at the Salvation Army's night shelter every Christmas. Thus began a tradition of volunteering that has continued for more than twenty years. Every Saturday night, the Appelgets and their now-grown children (and their spouses) gather at the Urban Ministry to prepare the evening meal for the homeless guests who will be spending the night there. Mrs. Appelget, a public health nurse, says, "I realized a long time ago that I couldn't save the world, but maybe I could make a difference." [8] That is a very powerful message indeed for parents to communicate to their children.

As is true of all aspects of character development, the parents' personal example is critical in teaching children to care and to serve. As children see their parents giving blood, voting, helping to build Habitat for Humanity houses, collecting funds for the March of Dimes, baking cookies for a school party, or visiting the bereaved, they absorb some valuable lessons about service. Even more important, however, is the genuine compassion and concern for others modeled in the parents' daily lives. At the heart of these lessons in caring and service is the relationship between and among family members. Obviously, children who feel cared about find it easier to care about others. Like charity, compassion begins at home.

In *The Measure of Our Success,* Marian Wright Edelman says that her parents and the members of her church taught the children of her community that no task was too lowly to do. They did this not by lecturing or sermonizing but by their own personal example. As a child of eight or nine years of age, Ms. Edelman heard her parents debating whether she was too young to accompany her older brother to help clean the bed and bedsores of an elderly woman who was very sick. "I went," she said, "and learned just how much the smallest helping hands and kindness can mean to a person in need." [9] For her and for her family, service was a way of life, and it spanned all ages.

There are many examples of kindness, compassion, and generosity that parents can share with their children. Obviously, the lives of people like Mother Teresa and Mahatma Gandhi serve as stellar examples of service, but there are also everyday people who are committed to making a difference in our world. One of these is Miss Oseola McCarty of Hattiesburg, Mississippi. This ninety-year-old woman, who left school at the age of twelve to help her family, recently assigned her life savings of $150,000 to fund scholarships for needy college students after her death. Miss McCarty earned the money as a laundress. Living a simple, frugal, and prayerful life, she walked to the bank each week, making deposits from her meager wages.

Miss McCarty's remarkable generosity has recently captured the attention of the media and the President of the United States, who awarded her the Presidential Citizens Medal. In her little book, *Simple Wisdom for Rich Living*, Miss McCarty says, "I think the way we live matters, not just for now but for always. There is an eternal side to everything you do."[10]

There is surely an eternal side to the work of parents. The way they live, the examples they provide, and the lessons they teach will have lasting effects on their children, their communities, and their world. The returns on these investments in the younger generation will not be monetary, but they will be priceless. Helen Keller once observed that "the best and most beautiful things in the world cannot be seen or even touched. They must be felt with the heart."[11] Such are the rewards for teaching children to care.

· · · · · · · · · · · · · · ·

[1] The Editors of *Guideposts*, *Turning Needs into Deeds* (Carmel, NY: Guideposts, 1995), p. 35.

[2] "The Day That Makes a Difference," *USA Weekend*, April 17-19, 1998, p. 4.

[3] Stephen Covey, *Principle-Centered Leadership* (New York: Simon & Schuster, 1992), p. 141.

[4] Robert J. Chaskin and Diana Mendley Rauner, "Youth and Caring," *Phi Delta Kappan*, May, 1995, p. 674.

[5] Stephen Covey, "The Guiding Conscience," *Handbook for the Soul*, ed. by Richard Carlson and Benjamin Shield (Boston: Little, Brown & Company, 1995), p. 150.

[6] Josephson Institute of Ethics, *Ethics in Action*, Fall, 1997, p. 7.

[7] Thomas Lickona, *Raising Good Children* (New York: Bantam Books, 1994), p. 26.

[8] Jim Schlosser, "Helping Others Runs in this Family," Greensboro (NC) *News and Record*, January 21, 1998.

[9] Marian Wright Edelman, *The Measure of Our Success* (Boston: Beacon Press, 1992), p. 4.

[10] Nancy Dorman-Hickson, "The Amazing Grace of Miss McCarty," *Southern Living*, February, 1998, pp. 33-34.

[11] The Editors of Conari Press, *Random Acts of Kindness* (Carmel, NY: Guideposts, 1993), p. 24.

Read to your children and keep good literature in the home.

In 1993, William Bennett published *The Book of Virtues: A Treasury of Moral Stories*. The book was an immediate success and enjoyed many weeks on the best-seller list. Why was (and is) the book so popular? It is a collection of the stories, poems, and myths which are a part of our culture—stories that teachers and parents of the past shared with each new generation, stories that helped mold and shape children's character and moral reasoning. In volumes like *The Book of Virtues*, modern readers are discovering anew that these stories are timeless and that they are just as relevant to today's moral issues as they were when our grandparents or great-grandparents were children.

In an era dominated by the electronic media, we seem to have forgotten that exposure to good literature is one of the most pleasant and least expensive ways to develop the moral literacy of children and youth. Francis Bacon once observed that if he could control the literature of the household, he would guarantee the well-being of the church and state. Similarly, George Washington advised parents to "cultivate literature and useful knowledge, for the purpose of qualifying the rising generation for patrons of good government, virtue, and happiness."[1]

Much earlier, Plato reminded adults in *The Republic* that it is in very early childhood that character is being formed and lasting impressions are made. He asks, "Shall we just carelessly allow children to hear any casual tales which may be devised by casual persons, and to receive into their minds ideas for the most part the very opposite of those which we should wish them to have when they are grown up?" We cannot do that, Plato warns, because "anything received into the mind at that age is likely to become indelible and unalterable; and therefore it is most important that the tales which the young first hear should be models of virtuous thoughts."[2] One could believe that Plato was referring to some of the disturbing ideas implanted in our youths' minds by television, movies, and music!

Books That Build Character: A Guide to Teaching Your Child Moral Values Through Stories, by William Kilpatrick and Gregory and Suzanne Wolfe, is one of the best resources for parents and teachers that I have seen. Not only do the authors provide a sound rationale for using literature to develop children's character, but they also include an extensive annotated bibliography by age level. Following Plato's reasoning, they caution, "If you as a parent don't take steps to educate your child's imagination, it's an almost sure bet that his imagination will be seduced by the power of popular culture."[3]

As indicated throughout this book, I strongly believe that the family is at the heart of any efforts to develop good character in children and youth. One of the best ways that parents can strengthen family ties and simultaneously teach sound moral principles is to read to—and with—their children. The earlier this shared reading begins, the better. (An added bonus is that children who are read to are generally more successful in school. In fact, one school superintendent said that if we could get parents to read to their preschool children for just fifteen minutes a day, "we could revolutionize the schools."[4] Also, a recent National Commission on Reading report stated that the single most important contribution parents can make toward their children's success in school is to read aloud to them.[5])

Few family times are more special to children than when an older family member reads to them or tells them a story. They cherish this time with their parents, and they enjoy the stories they hear.

For example, I recently heard about an eight-year-old who announced to his parents that he was proclaiming the following Saturday "Brother Appreciation Day." To celebrate the occasion, he was going to spend the entire day reading to and playing with his three-year-old brother. The older boy's unselfish attitude toward his brother is touching and says much about the lessons he has already learned about caring for family members. At the same time, it shows that *he* enjoys reading and being read to. For that reason, he could think of no finer gift to give to his brother.

Not only is "story time" or shared reading special for children, but it is also very pleasant for parents. Although it is sometimes difficult to find even fifteen minutes of quiet time, most parents place a high priority on reading to their children, especially at bedtime. The physical and emotional closeness of reading together fosters trust and openness. Consequently, children may be more willing to share their joys and their fears at such times. Through the youngsters' questions and comments about the stories, parents gain important insights into their children's concerns. Such times offer excellent opportunities for comforting, for clarifying, and for sharing. Few other human interactions are so tender or so memorable.

In addition, family reading offers a special opportunity to participate in a ritual that has been shared for generations; there is a sense of kinship with those who have gone before and those who are to come. Jim Trelease, author of *The Read-Aloud Handbook*, captures that feeling of family tradition and its value—not just to the individual family, but to the larger culture as well—when he explains why he read to his children:

> I read for one reason: *not* because of any education courses I took in college (I'd taken none as an English major) and *not* because the pediatrician told me to (he hadn't). I read because *my* father read to *me*. And because he'd read to me, when my time came I knew intuitively there is a torch that is supposed to be passed from one generation to the next. And through the countless nights of reading I began to realize that when enough of the torchbearers—parents and teachers—stop passing the torches, a culture begins to die.[6]

Obviously, it is not appropriate for parents (or teachers) to turn story time into an opportunity to lecture children or administer a dose of "moral medicine." Good literature can teach children important lessons even when they don't realize that they are learning. Consider, for example, *Number the Stars*, by Lois Lowry. This delightful book, which appeals to adults as well as children, is about a Christian family that protected a young Jewish girl during the Nazi occupation of Denmark. The daughter in the family is terrified when the Nazi soldiers barge in to search their home. She realizes that her Jewish friend is wearing a Star of David on her necklace. Quickly, she tears the chain from the other girl's neck and conceals it in her hand, squeezing so tightly that an image of the Star of David is imprinted on her palm.

One fourth grade teacher who read *Number the Stars* to her students witnessed the literal imprint that stories can make on children. To make the story real to her class, the teacher brought a Star of David to school and let the children pass the chain and sacred emblem around the room. While the teacher was reading, she found that all of the students pressed the star into their own palms, leaving a physical impression.[7] It is probably a safe assumption that those children will remember that book and its lessons about friendship and courage for the rest of their lives. Such experiences make lasting impressions, not just on the imagination, but on the heart and soul as well.

Good character involves three basic elements: A *knowledge* of what is good (understanding the meaning of virtues such as honesty, respect, and responsibility), a *desire* to do what is good (having a conscience, experiencing empathy for others, etc.) and a *willingness to act* based on what is good (putting moral principles into action). Good literature can be helpful in each of these areas. Novels, stories and poems, as well as biographies and autobiographies help children understand what the terms mean as they are played out in the lives of the literary characters. Carefully selected stories can also inspire children to want to do right and to apply those principles in their own lives. In essence, they give children a broader view of life and increase their understanding of the world. As Gladys Hunt, author of *Honey for a Child's Heart*, observed, "A good book has a profound kind of morality—not a cheap, sentimental sort which thrives on shallow plots and superficial heroes, but the sort of force which inspires the reader's inner life and draws out all that is noble."[8]

In addition to developing their imagination and moral sensitivity, reading to children can also help them cope with challenges in their own lives. There are excellent books available, for example, to help youngsters cope with the death of a family members, the frustrations of growing up, and the challenges of getting along with others. Also, books can help children and their parents transcend difficult circumstances. To illustrate, consider the following statement from a woman who rose above her poverty and is now a successful writer:

> I was raised in a big city. We were poor and didn't have a car, so we had little access to nature. At the row house where I grew up, there were very few trees or even greenery. But my grandmother used to tell me stories about her life on a farm. She read Walt Whitman, Emerson, and Thoreau to me. Sitting on her lap as a young girl, I was given the gift of a greater reality than the big cement city that was my world.[9]

William Bennett has devoted much time and energy to raising awareness of the character crisis in our nation and the need to return to teaching our children how to be people of virtue and honor. He believes—as do many others—that good literature provides an excellent means of passing on the moral legacy of our culture. Most Americans agree on certain principles of character, or virtues, such as honesty, compassion, and courage. However, children are not born knowing what these virtues are; they must be taught, and stories (such as those included in *The Book of Virtues*) offer an excellent means for doing so. Mr. Bennett outlines the following reasons for using literature to teach character:

- Stories give children some specific reference points.

- Stories are fascinating to children. (No one has improved on the opening line "Once upon a time. . . .")

- Stories help anchor our children in their culture, its history and traditions.

- In teaching these stories, we engage in an act of renewal [in which] we welcome our children to a common world, a world of shared ideals, to the community of moral persons.[10]

Great teachers, including Aesop, Socrates, Confucius, and Jesus, have always used stories as powerful means of instruction. The fables of Aesop, for example, are short and direct. At the end of each is a very clear moral. Similarly, Jesus used simple parables—not complex philosophical lectures—to teach his followers. For example, he could have delivered a lengthy sermon about the importance of loving one's neighbor and treating all people—even those who are different from us—with compassion and respect. Some of his audience would have understood; others would not. Instead, he told a story about a "Good Samaritan" and even the children could understand.

All of us, regardless of age or educational level, enjoy a good story. It captures our attention, draws us in, and engages both our intellect and our emotions. Consequently, audiences always tune in when a teacher, minister, or politician says, "That reminds me of a story. . . ." Developing in children a knowledge of what is good, a desire to be good, and the will to do good is an emotional as well as an intellectual activity, and stories provide the perfect bridge between the mind and the heart. It just makes sense, therefore, to use "the magic of literature" to "capture the imagination and to touch the heart" of the children whose character we are trying to develop.[11]

Most of us could name at least one book that has had a profound influence on our lives. When I taught English to high school students, I often had the privilege of witnessing first-hand the impact that literature can have on adolescents. As they grappled with the moral dilemmas of Pip in *Great Expectations,* examined the ethical issues in *Macbeth,* or considered the courage exhibited by Atticus Finch in *To Kill a Mockingbird,* they were developing their understanding of human relationships and of the world. Through these works and others, they were able to confront a wide range of character issues that had direct implications for their own lives. The same kind of experience can occur at almost any age level with age-appropriate literature.

Even graduate schools are re-discovering the power of stories as a teaching tool, and some are using literature to influence the ethics of aspiring leaders. At Harvard Business School, for example, child psychiatrist Robert Coles teaches an ethics course based entirely on stories and novels. Using carefully selected literary works, the graduate students explore "the gradual slope that leads to compromising one's principles, values, and morality." The objective of this teaching method, according to Dr. Coles, is "to bring the reader up close, so close that his empathy puts him in the shoes of the characters." Ultimately, he adds, "You hope when he closes the book his own character is influenced."[12] That same goal applies to the use of literature at any age as we attempt to influence individuals to become better human beings.

Although some of the language is outdated, the following selection by Strickland Gillilan, which appeared in the 1936 volume *Best Loved Poems of the American People,* still applies today. It captures the value of reading in the home and reminds us once more that "reading mothers" (*and reading fathers!*) pass on a meaningful and lasting moral legacy to their children.

THE READING MOTHER

I had a mother who read to me
Sagas of pirates who scoured the sea,
Cutlasses clenched in their yellow teeth,
"Blackbirds" stowed in the hold beneath.
I had a Mother who read me lays
Of ancient and gallant and golden days;
Stories of Marmion and Ivanhoe,
Which every boy has a right to know.
I had a Mother who read me tales
Of Gelert the hound of the hills of Wales
True to his trust till his tragic death,
Faithfulness blent with his final breath.

I had a Mother who read me the things
That wholesome life to the boy heart brings—
Stories that stir with an upward touch
Oh, that each mother of boys were such!
You may have tangible wealth untold;
Caskets of jewels and coffers of gold.
Richer than I you can never be—
I had a Mother who read to me.[13]

[1] *Leaves of Gold*, Williamsport, PA: (The Coslett Publishing Company, 1962), p. 63.

[2] William Bennett, *The Book of Virtues* (New York: Simon & Schuster, 1993), p. 17.

[3] William Kilpatrick and Gregory and Suzanne Wolfe, *Books That Build Character* (New York: Simon & Schuster, 1994), p. 22.

[4] Jim Trelease, *The New Read-Aloud Handbook* (New York: Penguin Books, 1989), p. xiii.

[5] Kilpatrick, Wolfe, and Wolfe, op. cit., p. 18.

[6] Jim Trelease, *The Read Aloud Handbook*, 4th ed. (New York: Penguin Books, 1995), p. xv.

[7] Ibid., p. 20.

[8] Gladys Hunt, *Honey for a Child's Heart* (Grand Rapids, MI: Zondervan Publishing House, 1989), p. 40.

[9] Linda Leonard, "Seasons of the Soul," *Handbook for the Soul*, Richard Carlson and Benjamin Shield, ed. (Boston: Little, Brown and Company, 1995), p.79.

[10] Bennett, *The Book of Virtues*, op. cit., p. 12.

[11] Thomas Lickona, *Raising Good Children*, (New York: Bantam Books, 1994), p. 345.

[12] Trelease, op. cit., pp. 58-59.

[13] Strickland Gillilan, "The Reading Mother," *The Best Loved Poems of the American People*, Hazel Felleman, ed. (Garden City, NY: Garden City Books, 1936), p. 376.

Limit your children's spending money. Help them appreciate non-material rewards.

L et me ask you a hypothetical question. Suppose that you are faced with the difficult situation in which you have to give your own child over to someone else to raise. You have two couples from whom to choose. The first are a poor mother and father, both of whom work, but they are barely able to make ends meet. Yet, they are impeccably honest, and they value education. For them, integrity and personal responsibility are high priorities.

Neither the husband nor wife in the second couple works, but they are financially "comfortable," having won a million-dollar lottery, guaranteeing them an annual income of $50,000 for life. In contrast to the first couple, they would be able to clothe your child nicely rather than relying on hand-me-downs. However, they do not value education, and are indifferent to issues of integrity and personal responsibility. Both couples would treat your child equally as well in terms of warmth and affection. Which would you choose?

The answer seems obvious—or so William Raspberry assumed when he posed this dilemma to a class of bright upperclassmen at Duke University, most of whom were from affluent homes. Thinking that the problem was a "no-brainer," Mr. Raspberry was prepared to add additional details to the story to make it more complicated and the decision more difficult. He didn't have to do that, however. For about half of the class, the choice was immediately clear; they said they would place the child in the care of the couple with more money. Why would they do this? One young man, apparently speaking for many of his classmates, said that because there are many places other than the home where children can learn values, he would choose economic security over character. In other words, having assured the child's material comfort, he was willing to "take his chances that his child would learn integrity and other positive values somewhere else—in school, in church or from neighbors."[1]

The response of these intelligent young adults seems to symbolize the materialistic attitudes of many Americans. Ours is a consumer-oriented culture, and from the time they are toddlers, our children are bombarded with messages that focus on financial comfort and social image—wearing brand-name clothing, living in the "right" neighborhood, and driving an expensive car. It should not surprise us, therefore, when our youth confuse shadow with substance and when they behave as if the ultimate goal in life is to accumulate more and more material goods.

Recognizing the economic power of the young, marketing specialists are targeting younger and younger children. In a *Business Week* article, "Hey Kid, Buy This!" David Leonhardt says that babies born today enter a "consumer culture, surrounded by logos, labels and ads almost from the moment of birth."[2] Even as infants leave the hospital, for example, their parents carry with them complimentary packages of items such as laundry detergent, disposable diapers, and baby lotion supplied by the manufacturers in the hope of selling more of these products.

By the time they are seven years old, today's babies will have watched an average of 20,000 commercials a year and will be active consumers. By age twelve, they will have their own entry in a marketer's data bank.

Through television, videos, Web sites, children's magazines, and displays in grocery and department stores, advertisers are attempting to influence the young to recognize brand names and to buy—or persuade their parents to buy—their products. Marketers who used to target parents are now going straight to the children. Why? According to one advertising executive, "We're relying on the kid to pester the mom to buy the product."[3] Also, because of the number of single- parent homes and the homes in which both parents work, many children are actually doing some of the shopping for the family. It is estimated that children aged fourteen and under directly spend *20 billion dollars* (combining allowances, earnings, and gifts) each year; they influence another *200 billion dollars* per year.[4] Obviously, they have great buying power.

Young adolescents, who are particularly insecure and concerned about fitting in, are especially susceptible to advertising hype. For them, brand-name clothing offers the "irresistible promise of instant cool."[5] So important is the label that it is often worn on the outside. Shunning less expensive, generic jeans or tee shirts, teenagers pay premium prices to wear Guess? or Tommy Hilfiger or Gap—or anything with a popular athlete's name or picture on it. In some instances, even parents who cannot afford it allow their children to buy these image clothes just to keep peace in the family—at least for the moment.

One mother, acknowledging the built-in obsolescence of greatly over-priced athletic shoes, rationalized, "At least you don't have any arguments and you've got a happy kid."[6] Unfortunately, this kind of parental behavior encourages selfishness on the part of the child and works against the development of good character. The net effect is that many of our youth have developed what psychologist Mary Pipher calls a "combination of narcissism, entitlement, and dissatisfaction."[7] It is that sense of entitlement that prompts some teenagers to rob or kill just to acquire the latest Nikes or a designer jacket. It also leads some youth to feel that they should have *anything* they want, without regard for the needs and wishes of others.

To capitalize on many teenagers' "I want what I want when I want it" attitudes, there are now banks, such as the Young Americans Bank in Denver that allow youth to borrow money, using allowances from their parents as income. Currently, about half of all sixteen- to nineteen-year-olds have part-time jobs. When allowance is combined with part-time earnings, the average youth in America has an income of about $64 per week. Do they save that money? Rarely—and if they do save, often it is to buy some high-cost item, such as tickets to a concert. As one writer expressed it, teenagers are "behaving like the fiscal equivalent of the Energizer Bunny. They keep spending and spending and spending."[8] For many, there is absolutely no accountability for the use of their funds.

We often read about the problems of poverty in our society and the need to address social problems stemming from poverty. However, there are also serious concerns related to affluence. Many of the troubling trends we see in youthful behavior (drugs, alcohol, materialism, promiscuity) are related to having *too much*—too much unsupervised time, too much freedom from responsibility, and too much money to spend as they wish. The cumulative effect of allowing our children to get caught up in today's "consumerist ethos" may be more profound than we realize.

David Leonhardt captures the unspoken concerns of many parents as he worries that "as kids drink in the world around them, many of their cultural encounters—from books to movies to TV—have become little more than sales pitches, devoid of any moral beyond a plea for a purchase." Rather than "transmitting a sense of who we are and what we hold important," he says, "today's marketing-driven culture is instilling in them the sense that little exists without a sales pitch attached and that self-worth is something you buy at a shopping mall."[9]

Lessons about money and its appropriate use are important components of character development. As is true of all efforts to help children become responsible and caring, our personal example in money matters is critical. Parents make strong statements about what they value by the ways they allocate their own resources, and by the ways they allow their children to spend the funds entrusted to them.

Some youth feel that any money they receive, whether an allowance, a gift, or a payment for work, is theirs to spend as they see fit. However, it seems reasonable for parents to set some limits on their children's spending. To help them understand budgeting, children should be expected to set aside a certain percentage of their funds for savings, clothing, charity, entertainment or other agreed-upon items. This practice will help them learn to set priorities, develop self-discipline, and delay gratification, as will requiring them to earn money and save for special purchases. By freely providing money whenever and for whatever children want, parents may unwittingly cause them to develop loose, irresponsible spending habits.

Often parents who have attained financial success say, "I want to give my children the things I didn't have when I was growing up. I don't want them to have to work. I want them to have it easier than I did." Consequently, they may actually be too generous in giving money and expensive gifts to their children. Even though their intentions are good, these parents seem to have forgotten that one reason *they* are successful is that they learned the value of sacrifice and hard work—that they were able to set goals and work to achieve them. They don't stop to consider, either, that giving a sixteen-year-old a new luxury car is not necessarily in the child's best interest. Children who receive unlimited funds and whose every wish is their parents' command will be ill-equipped for responsible adulthood.

Psychologist John Rosemond says that it is all parents' responsibility to teach their children a "fundamental, untransmutable law of reality." That law consists of three parts:

1. You cannot get your bread buttered on both sides.
2. There will be times when you won't be able to get it buttered on either side.
3. There will even be times when you won't have a piece of bread.[10]

Dr. Rosemond emphasizes that regardless of parents' income level, they should teach their children these principles. Instead of sharing their success with their children in limitless material ways, parents should share "the skills and values they will need to eventually achieve success on their own." He urges parents to practice the "Principle of Benign Deprivation." That is, teach your children how to set goals and work toward accomplishing them. By "depriving" them now (i.e., not automatically and indiscriminately granting all of their requests for money), you will better equip them to succeed in future.

Sometimes it seems there is a constant tug of war in progress for the hearts and minds of the young, with the homes, churches, and schools pulling and straining on one side while the negative influences of society tug with incredible strength on the other. How can we tilt the balance and counteract the materialism and the consumerism? As indicated throughout this book, one way to "inoculate" children against those influences is to instill strong moral values in them—through our words, deeds, and personal example.

Another way, according to Harriet Heath, author of *Planning: The Key to Meeting the Challenge of Parenting*, is for parents to give gifts to their children—not more Beanie Babies or cars or designer clothing, but gifts from the heart. What are those gifts? They are the "daily acts of love, support, and guidance that make an enormous difference in a child's life."[11] Through these gifts, we can help children understand that success is not based on what one *has* but what he or she *is* and help them find joy in the ordinary and the intangible.

- - - - - - - - - - - - -

[1] William Raspberry, "Do Kids Need Money or Values Most?" Washington Post Writers Group, reprinted in Greensboro (NC) *News and Record*, October 8, 1995.

[2] David Leonhardt, "Hey Kid, Buy This!" *Business Week*, June 30, 1997, p. 62.

[3] Ibid., p. 64.

[4] Ibid., p. 62.

[5] Ibid., p. 64.

[6] John Maher, "The Rising Cost of Cool," Austin (Texas) *American-Statesman*, August 13, 1995.

[7] Ibid., p. 63.

[8] David Fischer, "Let the Good Times Roll," *U. S. News and World Report*, July 1, 1996, p. 51.

[9] Leonhardt, op. cit., p. 63.

[10] John Rosemond, "Deprive Your Children," Burlington (NC) *Times News*, August 7, 1997.

[11] Nancy Kalish, "The Greatest Gifts We Can Give Our Children: A Report from the Ad Council," *Reader's Digest*, June, 1998.

Discuss holidays and their meanings. Have family celebrations and establish family traditions.

I n 1976, America had a year-long national celebration. To commemorate the two hundredth birthday of the United States, citizens across the country engaged in a public display of unabashed patriotism and thankfulness for freedom and democracy. Throughout the broadcast day during that year, television networks inserted a series of short biographical sketches of great Americans. Businesses, government buildings and private homes flew the American flag.

The celebration reached a climax on July 4th. The newly renovated Statue of Liberty was unveiled. Tall sailing ships from around the world converged in New York harbor. Concerts on the lawn filled municipal parks with patriotic music. Bright-eyed children sat on blankets with their parents, watching magnificent displays of red, white, and blue fireworks light up the summer sky. There was a feeling of national pride and hope that was almost palpable.

Celebrations played out not only in Washington and New York and Philadelphia, but also were replicated in small towns and communities all across America in the form of family picnics, block parties, and neighborhood parades. It seemed a good time to reflect on our freedom and to appreciate those who paved the way for our nation's success, and many families made pilgrimages to Independence Hall, Plymouth Rock, Ellis Island, or other historic sites. Few American homes were untouched by this meaningful and memorable celebration. It was a time for reflecting, for remembering, and for renewing commitments to our communities and our country.

Participating in a national bicentennial is a once-in-a-lifetime experience, but there are many other opportunities to celebrate the national and religious holidays, and we need to make them a part of our own family traditions. Why are such observances important in family life and in the development of good character? Abraham Lincoln provided an appropriate answer more than a century ago. Reflecting on the value of Independence Day celebrations, he said, "We go from these meetings in better humor with ourselves, we feel more attached, the one to the other, and more firmly bound to the country we inhabit."

Developing that feeling of attachment to and kinship with others is the major reason for teaching children about the meaning of holidays and for having family celebrations and traditions. Learning lessons early in life about respect and reverence and honor help to prepare our youth to be good citizens and people of good character. That is, if they feel connected and grounded at home, it will be much easier for them to feel a part of and responsible to the larger community. These holidays and traditions are a special kind of glue which binds us together as human beings, as family members, and as citizens. They also provide some of our most cherished memories.

To illustrate, close your eyes and think about your own childhood. What do you remember most fondly? What mental snapshots do you see? For the vast majority of adults, I expect that family celebrations would be most prominent. Perhaps it was your family's observance of Christmas or Hanukkah—the taste and aroma of special foods, the gathering of family and friends, the time of celebration. Or maybe it was a the way your parents made you feel special on your birthday or the day you first "soloed" on your bicycle or the celebration of your confirmation or bar mitzvah. Such memories provide a link back to our childhood and allow us to relive warm and happy times. They also enhance our sense of self-worth and our sense of belonging, not only to a family, but to a larger community as well.

These traditions and celebrations are a part of who we are, and they link us in unique ways to our families. They become part of each family's "story"—that family history that is passed from one generation to another. Because it is within the family that we learn much of the meaning of life, such stories are vital to children's development. So important are they, according to the authors of *Books that Build Character,* that "if there is no family story to pass on, if the family is not tied to some larger tradition, history, or religious story, children are not likely to gain much perspective on their lives."[1]

Most families have special ways of celebrating traditional holidays. Although there may be variations from year to year, the basic format is the same. In some families, for example, Christmas means caroling in the neighborhood, a midnight communion service, or cross-country visits to grandparents' homes. In a world of constant change and uncertainty, these traditions provide some comfort in their sameness and predictability. They become something that all family members can count on. They serve as a bridge of continuity from one year to another and unite family members in a common bond. Obviously, not all family celebrations resemble Norman Rockwell paintings, nor do they need to. Their real value lies not in appearances, but in their meaning to the family members involved.

Author and business consultant Stephen Covey says that family traditions "help you understand who you are: that you are part of a family that's a strong unit, that you love one another, that you respect and honor one another, that you celebrate one another's birthdays and special events, and make positive memories for everyone."[2] Through these traditions, he says, families give children a "feeling of belonging, of being supported, and of being understood."[3]

Memories of these special occasions become a kind of "strength insurance" to help family members through times of conflict or difficulty.[4] This premise was recently brought home to one of my friends whose husband had left the family and subsequently remarried. Not surprisingly, the family experienced considerable turmoil as they dealt with the drastic changes in their lives. Several years later, thinking that her teenage sons had outgrown the annual ritual of dyeing Easter eggs, the mother decided to drop that task from her spring agenda. However, when she told her younger son, he protested, so once again she boiled eggs and gathered all of the dyeing paraphernalia. Several of her son's friends happened to stop by, and they good-naturedly teased the young man about dyeing Easter eggs. Before the mother knew what was happening, however, her kitchen was full of teenage boys, happily participating in that family's tradition—a tradition that will probably be continued when that son has a family of his own.

Newspaper columnist Lucia Herndon wrote in a November 1997 article, "The holidays are approaching, but I've already received the best present."[5] What was the present? Her two "near-adult" children had asked her to return to family traditions they had given up when the children seemed to outgrow them, traditions like making candy and fudge for the neighbors and preparing special dishes that their grandmother used to cook for the holidays. Acknowledging that her children's request meant extra shopping and extra expense, more time and more cooking, she said, "But my heart is so happy. Happy to know that the kids actually did enjoy our time together when they were little." Then she added, "It also makes me happy to know that no matter how old they get or how far away from home they travel, they will have warm memories of our holiday times as a family. For that I am truly thankful."

The common theme running through this book is that there are many competing influences on the character of our children and youth. Eileen Kindig captures that concern as she cautions, "If ever there was a time when we needed to reclaim our identity, clarify our values and make memories with our children, it is now."[6] Sharing family stories, family celebrations, and family traditions are ways to "make memories with our children." They are also valuable components of the moral heritage we bequeath to the young.

[1] James Kilpatrick, Gregory Wolfe, and Suzanne Wolfe, *Books That Build Character* (New York: Simon & Schuster, 1994), p. 50.

[2] Stephen Covey, *The 7 Habits of Highly Effective Families* (New York: Golden Books, 1997), p. 280.

[3] Ibid.

[4] Jeane Westin, *The Coming Parent Revolution* (Bantam Books: New York, 1981), p. 241.

[5] Lucia Herndon, "Children Seek Return of Holiday Tradition," Knight-Ridder News Service, reprinted in Burlington (NC) *Times News*, November 27, 1997.

[6] Eileen S. Kindig, "Tell Me a Story," *Reader's Digest*, May, 1998, p. 166.

Capitalize on the "teachable moment." Use situations to spark family discussions on important issues.

ood habits are not made on birthdays, nor Christian charac-ter at the new year. The workshop of character is everyday life. The uneventful and commonplace hour is where the battle is lost or won."[1] These words of Maultbie D. Babcock remind us that some of the most effective character education can occur in the ongoing, ordinary life of the family. As parents and children interact with one another and with others outside the home, there are count-less situations which can be used to teach valuable lessons about goodness and morality. Just as teachers often depart from their planned curriculum to address a classroom situation or current hap-pening in order to teach a more important lesson about life, parents can also capitalize on these "teachable moments."

Children's conflicts with their siblings or friends and their com-ments about what happened at school, on the bus or the playground, or in the neighborhood provide opportunities for parents to gain understanding of what their children think about important issues and to help shape and mold that thinking. Often, it takes only a few comments to help the children recognize the character issues involved in their behavior (or that of others) and to reflect on how their actions and attitudes affect other people. These brief interactions can impart valuable lessons about empathy, kindness, tolerance, and compassion. The same is true of jokes children tell and stories they share, as well as movies or television programs which the family watches together, articles which appear in the newspaper or magazines, or situations which the family encounters in the mall or a restaurant, at an athletic event, or on the highway.

Consider, for example, an incident that attracted national media attention in 1996. Twelve-year-old Samuel Graham, of Fort Lauderdale, Florida, was often the brunt of his classmates' jokes because of his obesity. At 5 feet 4 inches and 174 pounds, he stood out from the other kids, and they taunted him in hateful, hurtful ways. In fact, the remarks were so painful to Samuel that he told relatives that he would rather die than endure more taunts. On the night before he was to enroll at Parkway Middle School, he said his prayers with his two younger brothers before going to bed. Later that night, he hanged himself from a tree in the backyard.[2]

Children can be very cruel to one another—and especially so during the middle school years. It is ironic that at the very time when they are intensely sensitive to anything that sets them apart or makes them stand out from their peers, they can taunt and tease one another so unmercifully. From experience with many students in the public schools, I don't believe that most really intend to inflict such deep wounds on others. Rather, the more typical problem is that they get caught up in the group's mood and they *just don't think*— they don't stop to consider how the other person feels. It is our task to help them learn to think before acting, to consider the effects of their behavior, and to treat others with empathy, respect, and compassion.

By discussing a newspaper article or television report such as the one about Samuel Graham, parents can help their children analyze such behavior more objectively and perhaps more thoughtfully than if they were directly involved. Such discussions allow family members to explore issues such as "What do you think?" "How would you feel—if you were Samuel, or Samuel's parents or younger brothers?" "How do you think the kids who teased Samuel felt?" and "What would you have done?" By asking questions and respectfully allowing children and teenagers to express their thoughts rather than simply delivering a sermon, parents will find that the discussion will have more meaning and greater effect. Frequently adults who engage in such conversations are surprised at the thoughtfulness that even young children can show and the empathy they express.

Ideally, these informal, everyday discussions will carry over into the children's behavior and be incorporated into their character. I heard about an incident that occurred in a middle school in North Carolina that lends support for this proposition. The seventh-graders had been studying a "heroes" unit about Raoul Wallenberg, a Swede who risked his life to save more than 100,000 Jews during the Holocaust. One day, one of their classmates came to school wearing a jacket over his pajamas. As kids will sometimes do, they began to tease the child about his clothing. This continued for several minutes, but then one student in the group spoke up and said, "I don't believe Raoul Wallenberg would act like this." With those words, the mood of the group changed completely. They learned that the boy was dressed that way because his family's home had burned during the night, and he had no other clothes. Immediately, the class rallied around the youngster, making understanding and supportive remarks. They also began a campaign to gather clothing for the youth and his family.

In *The Moral Intelligence of Children*, Robert Coles says that if we are to bring up children with "some moral success," we must "bring up matters of conscience, of ethical concern, again and again."[3] Reminding us that the conscience—or good character—does not descend from on high, Dr. Coles asserts that children learn a true sense of right and wrong from "parents who are themselves convinced as to what ought to be said and done and under what circumstances, as to what is intolerable, not at all permissible"— parents who are always at the ready to teach their children through their words and their daily example what they believe to be right. Without such parents, he says, a child's conscience is "not likely to grow up strong and certain."[4]

Once parents become aware of the "teachable moments," they find that there is material all around them for building children's character. An excellent example of a situation which parents could use to explore their children's thoughts and to communicate their own sense of "what is intolerable and not at all permissible" was reported across the nation last year. On the third day of Hanukkah, three teenage vandals in Pennsylvania broke the living room window of a Jewish family in their community, smashing their menorah and setting off fears of anti-Semitism. As a show of support, the victims' neighbors—most of whom were Christian—displayed a menorah in almost every window on the block.

Although the jury acquitted the youths of ethnic intimidation because they felt that anti-Semitism was not the motive, they found them guilty of criminal mischief and night prowling. Concerned that the teenagers might have missed the potential seriousness of their vandalism, the judge gave them an unusual sentence instead of sending them to jail. What did he do? He ordered them to watch the movie *Schindler's List*, write an essay on anti-Semitism, and also complete 250 hours of community service. One of the youths, who chose to do his community service at the local synagogue, apparently learned a valuable lesson. Of the incident, he said, "I hurt people. Now I want to do something to make up for it."[5]

An anecdote such as this could prompt serious and meaningful discussion around the dinner table. Once again, it could be used to help children—especially teenagers—understand the dangerous effects of acting without considering the consequences, and it could further develop their empathy for others. The same kinds of issues relate to other hate crimes and discrimination against those who are different in race, religion, social status, or physical appearance.

The moral development of children occurs slowly, and it is natural for them to have periods of doubt and confusion. Rather than blaming them for relapses or confusion, we need to provide them with many opportunities to think through important issues and ideas with adults whom they respect. Dr. Coles says that the young have a natural hunger and thirst for morality, and they seek to find it on their own and through the help of adults. There are many formal, direct ways in which parents can teach lessons about goodness and morality, but ultimately our most powerful and persuasive messages may be communicated during those "unselfconscious moments" in a child's life that we think of as "the unfolding events of the day and week."[6] We should all be prepared to recognize and respond to those "teachable moments." Perhaps at no other time will our lessons have greater impact.

[1] Mautlbie D. Babcock, quoted in *The Treasure Chest*, Charles L. Wallis, ed. (New York: Harper & Row Publishers, 1965), p. 45.

[2] Rosemary Yardley, "A Young Boy's Suicide," Greensboro (NC) *News and Record*, August 28, 1998.

[3] Robert Coles, *The Moral Intelligence of Children* (New York: Random House, 1997), p. 9.

[4] Ibid., p. 58.

[5] "Menorah-smashing Teens Spared Jail," Burlington (NC) *Times News*, June 8, 1997.

[6] Coles, op. cit., p. 31.

Strategy Fourteen

Assign home responsibilities to *all* family members.

When Albert Gore, son of the Vice President of the United States, was six years old, he darted in front of a car and was seriously injured as his father watched in horror and helplessness. The child suffered crushed internal organs and multiple broken bones. When he returned home after an extended stay in the hospital, he was in a body cast and required around-the-clock attention. His parents turned their dining room into a sick room and maintained a constant vigil at Albert's bedside.

Attempting to shield Albert's three older sisters from anxiety, the parents told them not to worry—that everything was fine. Shouldering the full load of Albert's care, they did not involve the other children at all. After a while, however, they realized that their exclusion of Albert's siblings was a mistake. They gradually understood that the girls *wanted* to help care for their brother, so they changed their routine. No longer did the parents take turns staying up all night to turn their son at regular intervals. Instead, they set the alarm and let the other children do it.

"That's what they wanted," Mrs. Gore explained. By helping take care of Albert, they felt involved. Rather than simply observing helplessly, they were able to *do* something. They were able to help their family in a time of crisis. "They felt such pain about what he was going through," their mother said. "It was better to give them a positive role to play in his healing even though that was a little hard on them. They had to wake up maybe a little sleepy for school the next day, but it was so much better."[1]

The Gores' experience illustrates an important point about giving children meaningful responsibilities in the home. Most children *want* to help and want to be involved in the family in meaningful ways, and it is in the home that we learn our most lasting lessons about caring for others, placing others' welfare and comfort before our own, and contributing through service to our homes and to the larger society. Such lessons are major building blocks of character.

One of my best friends summarizes her approach to child-rearing as the "Mack truck philosophy." That is, she tried to prepare her children to function independently so that if she were hit by a Mack truck, they would be able to carry on and function independently. Her children, now grown and successful, are a fine testament to that method of preparing children for responsible adulthood. Vera White, principal of an inner-city middle school in Washington, D.C. espouses a similar approach, stating that her goal is to help her students become "independently capable of doing the right thing." Innate in both approaches is the belief that children are capable of assuming responsibility for their own behavior and for making meaningful contributions to the home and school.

In Colonial times, families had no choice but to assign responsibilities to the young. All family members, including very young children, were expected to help with housekeeping and meal preparation, work in the fields, milk the cows and gather the eggs, and assist in the care of the sick or infirm. On farms today, it is not unusual to see children carrying out very responsible roles. Because the family's economic health depends on the efforts of all members, children and youth know that their contributions matter. Whether driving a tractor, helping with the harvest, or cooking meals for the field hands, they develop both confidence and character as they meet daily challenges.

The Amish seem particularly aware of the need to involve children in meaningful activities. In part, it is a matter of character, but it is also a necessity because their non-mechanized agrarian lifestyle requires the help of *all* family members. On several occasions, I have had an opportunity to observe the interactions of Amish families and have been impressed by the responsibilities they entrust to their youth. It is not unusual, for example, to see young boys working in the fields, shoulder-to-shoulder with older relatives, or driving teams of horses to harvest or bale the hay. Young girls help their mothers plant and tend the immaculate vegetable and flower gardens, assist with household chores, and even work in the fields as conditions require. Without benefit of electricity or machinery, the Amish need their children, and their children sense both their value and their responsibility to the family. That sense of responsibility also extends to the larger community as whole families—from children to grand-parents—join together in "barn-raisings" or other activities to help neighbors in need.

Unlike farmers, most parents today do not work at home. Because urban family life is generally less labor-intensive than farm life, we tend to lose sight of the importance of giving children opportunities to contribute to the functioning of the home. Over-all, we Americans tend to expect very little from our children. Far too many parents shield their children from any responsibility for routine household tasks. In some ways, parents treat their children and teenagers like members of athletic team who are never allowed to get into the game. They simply warm the bench, passively observing while their parents shoulder all of the meaningful tasks. The result is that parents unwittingly deprive their children of many opportunities to feel important and competent and to savor the satisfaction of a job well done.

Psychologist and author John Rosemond speaks to thousands of parents every year. One exercise he uses with large groups is to ask parents to raise their hands if they expect their children to do routine chores in the home—for which the children receive no pay (including an allowance). Typically, in an audience of five hundred, no more than fifty people will raise their hands. He then asks the audience to raise their hands if *their* parents would have raised their hands in response to the same question. This time, people begin to laugh and almost all raise their hands. This brief activity, Rosemond says, illustrates that in just one generation, we have lost sight of an important principle of child-rearing—that "children should be *contributing* members of their families."[2] Even though it is often easier to clear the table, take out the trash, or load the dishwasher ourselves than to wait for a child to do it, we have an obligation to help children learn to balance their own selfish needs against those of other family members—and ultimately, other members of society.

Common sense and personal experience tell us that the more we are involved in any group or organization, the more we value our membership. That is certainly true of the family. In addition to boosting children's self-confidence by giving them a sense of accomplishment, chores help to bond them to the values of the family, especially when they work with other family members on joint projects, such as cleaning out the garage, painting a room, or landscaping the yard. By contributing to their families on a regular basis through meaningful chores, children "come to a clearer understanding of their parents' values."[3] In other words, by feeling invested in and valued by the family, children are more likely to pattern their own attitudes and behavior after those of their parents.

Moral reasoning and moral behavior are the major objectives of character education. Developmental psychologist Thomas Lickona says that we can help children grow in both of these areas by giving them *real* responsibilities. Just as respect begets respect, responsibility begets responsible behavior. If we want children to become responsible, we need to give them meaningful duties in the home. Especially important are responsibilities that involve caring for others and making some "tangible contribution to the welfare of other human beings."[4] Such activities might include supervising or reading to a younger brother or sister, sharing the housework, helping with gardening or yard work, or assuming responsibility for the care of a pet. Whatever the duties, if approached properly, they can help children develop responsibility, dependability, compassion, self-discipline, effective time-management, and a positive work ethic.

In many ways, the home is a microcosm of society, and it provides an excellent place to develop good citizenship. John Rosemond paraphrases John Kennedy's "Ask not what your country can do for you but ask what you can do for your country." He says that children should be taught to consider what they can do for their families, rather than being passive, selfish consumers. The family, says Dr. Rosemond, should require of children what the community will eventually require of them—honesty, responsibility, respect for others, a willingness to share, [and] industriousness." Consequently, "those social values must also be family values, and they must be as much a part of the child's daily life as three balanced meals."[5]

A teacher in a high school serving a high percentage of affluent, academically talented adolescents told me recently that the faculty has a difficult time getting the students to pick up after themselves in the cafeteria and halls. Their attitude, she said, is "We pay people to take care of things like that." This is a sad commentary on the values these youth have acquired. Despite their scholastic success, they have failed miserably in their lessons on responsibility. Somehow they have missed the important message that responsibility is a form of respect that we owe to others and that it summons us to try "to nurture and support each other, alleviate suffering, and make the world a better place for all."[6]

As we attempt to instill in our youth a sense of citizenship and responsibility, an ever-present challenge is to help them find a balance between their own needs and the needs of others. In the 1960s, at the height of the era of "*my* rights and *my* feelings," psychiatrist and Auschwitz survivor Viktor Frankl proposed the construction of a Statue of Responsibility on the West Coast to serve as a balance to the Statue of Liberty on the East Coast.[7] The symbolism has a message for character development.

If we never ask children to help, if we never give them any real responsibility, if we never involve them in any kind of caring relationship with others, and if we expect nothing of them except the pursuit of their own comfort and happiness, we cannot hope that they will find that balance. On the other hand, if we expect each family member to provide service to the home, we will help children and youth see beyond their own selfish interests and to develop "an enduring orientation toward the common good."[8] If we do these things, we will enable them to understand that happiness does not lie in freedom *from* responsibility and to appreciate the truth in the adage that *real joy comes not from ease or riches or from the praise of men, but from doing something worthwhile.*[9]

[1] Tamara Jones, "The National Nurturer," *Good Housekeeping,* July, 1998, p. 113.

[2] John Rosemond, *Six-Point Plan for Raising Happy, Healthy Children* (Kansas City: Andrews & McMeel, 1997), p. 81.

[3] Ibid., p. 82.

[4] Thomas Lickona, *Raising Good Children,* (New York: Bantam Books, 1994), p. 25.

[5] John Rosemond, "Volunteering for Kids," *The Rotarian,* March, 1996, p. 116.

[6] Thomas Lickona, *Educating for Character: How Our Schools Can Teach Respect and Responsibility* (New York: Bantam Books, 1992), p. 44.

[7] Viktor E. Frankl, *Man's Search for Meaning* (New York: Pocket Books, 1963), pp. 209-210.

[8] William Damon, *The Youth Charter,* (New York: The Free Press, 1997), p. 77.

[9] W. T. Grenfell, quoted in *The Treasure Chest,* Charles L. Wallis, ed., (New York: Harper & Row, 1965), p. 153.

Set clear expectations for your children and hold them accountable for their actions.

O ne of my first clients as a high school counselor was a bright, witty, and articulate young woman I will call Sandy. She was a good student and was well liked by her teachers and classmates. What then was Sandy's problem? Her well-kept secret was that both of her parents were alcoholics. Because of their own problems, they had little time to be concerned about hers.

Sandy's parents were very permissive. They gave her a car and spending money and allowed her to make most of her decisions on her own. Occasionally, they would give her some direction, such as telling her what time they wanted her to come home on weekend nights. Sandy soon realized that it didn't matter whether she paid any attention to their restrictions. "I can come in whenever I want, and they won't care—*if* they even know when I come home." Sobbing, she said, "I just wish I had someone who cared enough to get upset when I don't do what they say."

Contrast Sandy's situation with that of another teenager I know. Rick (not his real name) was sixteen and had just gotten his driver's license. His single mother was concerned about his safety as a new driver. She made her expectations clear and told Rick what time she expected him to be home on school nights, which also happened to be work nights for her. On the very first night that he took the car out on his own, Rick succumbed to peer pressure and poor judgment and came in more than two hours late. Not only did he not call to let his mother know that he was going to be late, but he also brought several friends home with him, knowing that he—or his mother—would have to go out again to take them home.

Rick's mother was very worried and very tired by the time her son returned. Although she had been allowing him to drop her off at work and drive her car to school, she immediately grounded her son. She returned to her practice of taking him to school and requiring him to ride the bus home in the afternoons—a real setback for one who was so proud of his new independence. The mother also talked at length with her son about the lack of respect and concern for others that he had shown. She told him how worried she was—fearing that he had been in an accident—and tried to help him to understand the seriousness of his behavior. Finally, she told him that he would have to earn her trust again by exhibiting responsibility in other areas before he could drive again.

Was this a calm domestic discussion in which the son said, "I see your point, Mom. I realize what a selfish, inconsiderate person I've been, and your actions are perfectly reasonable"? Hardly. The son became very emotional, told his mother that she was overreacting, and refused to speak to her the next morning. After a sullen ride to school, he got out of the car without even saying good-bye. (This behavior came from a usually affectionate, respectful teenager.)

By the time the mother returned home from work, she and her son had had time to think about the incident. It had been a miserable day for both. The mother, who was deeply hurt by her son's reaction, found herself questioning whether she had been too harsh. "It would be a lot easier," she said "to just let him do whatever he wants." The son, much to her relief, had come to understand his mother's position. As they talked late into the evening, Rick acknowledged her concerns and his own mistakes. This time, he said, "I hate to admit it, but you were right, Mom, and I was wrong.

I'm sorry." Despite his apology, however, the suspension of driving privileges remained in effect for a month.

The mother in the second anecdote illustrates the importance of setting reasonable limits for children and enforcing those limits. The outcome was not a result of blind luck or Rick's superior moral reasoning. Rather, it was just one piece of a family mosaic made of many discussions about the mother's expectations of her son. Because of his previous relationship with his mother, Rick realized that she had his best interest at heart. He understood—reluctantly at first—that when she imposed a restriction, she had a good reason. He also knew that she would hold him accountable if he violated her trust. In other words, he understood that his mother personified the expression: *Say what you mean and mean what you say.*

Some parents resist imposing rules or consequences for their children's conduct. For example, the parent of a three-year-old said, "I'm not going to lay a power trip on my child. She is her own person. If she wants to eat nothing but Hostess Twinkies for breakfast, lunch, and dinner, that will be her decision."[1] This father obviously didn't want anyone telling him what to do, so he intended to extend the same courtesy to his preschooler. Somehow he missed the point that children are not ready to take on the independence of adulthood and are not prepared to make their own decisions about diet *or* behavior without their parents' guidance and direction.

Jeane Westin, author of *The Coming Parent Revolution*, spent several years studying parent-child relationships. She collected opinions and personal experiences of parents representing more than 400 families. When she asked the parents of grown or nearly grown children what they would change if they were rearing their children over again, *increased discipline* was the single most frequent answer. Parents made statements like "I'd insist my teenagers accept more responsibility for their actions" and "I'd hang on tighter, longer, and be tougher."[2]

Interestingly, Mrs. Westin's book was published in 1981. Those parents would have been rearing their children during the permissiveness of the 1960s and 1970s. The author observed that because the emphasis of the era was on parents' listening to children rather than children paying attention to their parents, there was a kind of "paralysis of discipline." Giving in to their children's demands and accepting outrageous behavior, some parents were "understanding" themselves into immobility.[3] Unfortunately, remnants of that philosophy still influence parent-child relationships in some homes.

Most parents will readily admit that the most difficult years of child rearing come during adolescence. Precariously straddling the conflicting worlds of childhood and adulthood, youth often engage in behavior that is puzzling to their parents and to themselves. In their quest for independence, they challenge authority, especially that of their parents. They want to be independent—to be their own persons; yet, they compliantly conform to the dress and language of their peers, trying to blend in with the crowd. Because of concern with themselves and their changing bodies, they sometimes behave selfishly; at other times they exhibit incredibly altruistic attitudes. Typically, adolescents take risks, believing that illness, death, and tragedy affect other people but not them. Because they are young and presumably have their whole lives ahead of them, they may feel that they are immortal.

It is little wonder that the parent-child relationship is often a turbulent and trying one, to say the least. One moment, the teenager is a reasonable, considerate person; the next, he may be a sullen, rebellious stranger. For parents to have a good relationship with their teenagers, they must begin laying the foundation when the children are infants. Even as babies, children need the security of knowing that there is order in their world. As very young children, they need to learn basic lessons about sharing, helping in the home and showing respect for others. Parents who lovingly and firmly set limits on their children's behavior are helping to socialize the children not only as family members, but as good citizens and responsible members of the larger society as well.

It is very important that parents teach their children the cause-and-effect relationship of their behaviors. For example, if a child hits a playmate, he or she needs to understand that it hurts the other child. Also, parents should impose some reasonable consequence for the inappropriate conduct. At a minimum, the child needs to make some form of restitution—at least an apology. Such lessons are critical to the development of the conscience. Also, children who learn to control their behavior in minor ways will be far more likely to show self-discipline and self-control in more serious situations they face in later life, especially during the teenage years.

In my work in the schools and community, I have seen many youngsters whose lives were really messed up because of poor decisions related to drugs, alcohol, and sex. Therefore, I cannot over-emphasize the importance of parents' communicating their expectations clearly and unequivocally in these areas. Simply stated, parents need to help their children understand the risks to their health and safety, help them rehearse appropriate reactions to peer pressure, and let them know what the consequences for violation of the rules will be.

A recent issue of *Time* magazine carried a shocking account of American teenagers' cavalier attitudes toward sex and their numerous liaisons, often with people they hardly know. The article prompted many letters to the editor, including one from a parent in Texas. The writer said that he had come home earlier than expected one day and found his son and his girlfriend (both fifteen years old) having unprotected sex in the family's backyard hot tub. The music was blasting, and the teenagers were drinking wine. The parent's reaction? "The next day I bought my son condoms."[4]

In that home, there was apparently a breakdown in communication about acceptable behavior. Unfortunately, the parent's response illustrates the mixed messages our society is sending to our youth about sex and about alcohol. Insofar as alcohol is concerned, some parents tell their children not to drink, but they make beer, wine, and liquor accessible to them. Likewise, some parents tell their children that they should not engage in sexual relations before marriage; yet, they provide them with condoms or birth control pills. The implication is "You shouldn't do this, but we know you can't control yourself, so at least use protection."

This view loses sight of the larger issues—the character issues—of responsible behavior, self-control, and respect for oneself and for others. It fails to teach the lesson that it is wrong to use other people, and it misses the point that the dangers of casual sex go beyond the possibility of pregnancy, AIDS, or other sexually transmitted diseases—although these issues are sabotaging our youths' future at alarming rates. An even greater toll lies in the damage to self-esteem and the psychological pain that teenagers experience when they lose self-respect or feel that they have been used. As Dr. Thomas Lickona says, there is no birth control barrier large enough to protect the heart.

One of the most difficult challenges of parenting is to find the proper balance between permissiveness and strictness. When parents are overly strict, their children are more likely to rebel and to push the limits when they do get a taste of freedom. On the other hand, children whose parents set no limits may be expected to engage in some risky behaviors, to say the least. The critical balance is to set "firm and loving limits" that protect children, especially teenagers, while still allowing them some of the freedom which they seek.[5]

It is especially important for children to perceive their parents' restrictions as reasonable and fair. That is far more likely to happen if parents take time to explain why the rules are important and to set the rules and consequences within the context of their love and concern for their children. Defining limits and enforcing them appropriately establishes the parents as the moral leaders in the home and provides a sense of security to children and youth. It also lets them know that they are important to you and that you care enough to want them to be—or to become—good people.

My father often said, "You know right from wrong, and I expect you to show it." He understood—as do many parents—that having high expectations means that you have confidence that your children are capable of living up to those expectations. That is one of the finest compliments that you can pay to your children.

[1] Thomas Lickona, "Character Development in the Family," *Character Development in the Schools and Beyond*, edited by K. Ryan and T. Lickona (Washington, DC: The Council for Research in Values and Philosophy, 1992), p. 203.

[2] Jeane Westin, *The Coming Parent Revolution* (NY: Bantam Books, 1981), p. 162.

[3] Ibid.

[4] "Letters," *Time*, July 6, 1998, p. 20.

[5] Kristine Napier, *The Power of Abstinence* (New York: Avon Books, 1996), p. 186.

Keep your children busy in positive activities.

C hildren have remarkable energy levels. They can be wonderfully spontaneous and creative, and the challenge for parents is to channel that energy in positive ways. Involving youth in constructive activities such as hobbies, sports, music, service projects, or scouting can serve several major purposes. First, and most obvious, is the elimination of large amounts of unstructured, unsupervised time reduces the likelihood that youngsters will simply while away their time in front of the TV set or occupy themselves with inappropriate activities such as experimenting with drugs, alcohol, or sex. Parents of previous generations believed that "idle hands are the devil's workshop." The adage still applies.

Second, such activities add meaning and pleasure to life. People of all ages want and need to be productive. Even toddlers assert, "I can do it myself," and they beam with pride at their simplest accomplishments. Psychologist William James asserted that the deepest principle in human nature is the craving to be appreciated. I believe that there is an equally deep desire to feel competent. For all of us, there is a certain joy and affirmation that comes from doing something well—from experiencing the satisfaction of learning new skills, developing one's own unique talents, or gaining competence in a particular area.

As children and youth work through the trials and frustrations of mastering a creative or competitive skill, they not only become more accomplished and resourceful, but their self-confidence and their self-esteem also increase. Psychiatrist William Glasser says that the more youngsters "are able to do on their own, or with occasional parental help but a lot of parental interest, the stronger they will be."[1] That strength will enable them to go forward to new challenges with faith in their ability to do a job and do it well.

Consider for example, the sense of accomplishment which Mance Minton, a youngster in my community, experienced when he used skills developed through his hobby to set up a computer learning center in a facility for disadvantaged youth. The ninth-grader, who showed a special interest in and knack for electronics when he was only four years old, undertook the project as a part of his efforts to earn the Eagle Scout award. Mance wrote letters to local businesses and placed advertisements in the newspaper and in his church bulletin, requesting donations of used computer equipment.

Over about a five-month period which included his summer vacation, Mance sorted through the donations, set up the computers, and installed the software. Then he undertook the task of teaching basic computer skills to the youngsters attending the center. When asked what he is proudest of, he says without hesitation, "Going into the center and watching the kids using the computers and learning. It's really something."

Mance admits that there were times when he felt overwhelmed and wondered whether he would be able to complete the task. Then he adds, "I learned that you can do anything if you put your mind to it." Although he has completed the project requirements for the Eagle Scout award, the fourteen-year-old is continuing his involvement with the center. He is still seeking donations of hardware as area businesses purchase new equipment. His present goal? To upgrade all of the computers in the youth center.[2] For this fine young man, the project is clearly about more than earning a personal award. It represents a commitment to invest his own time, energy, and talents in those who are less fortunate.

Mance Minton's story illustrates two important kinds of purposeful activities—hobbies and scouting—and the benefits of each. As psychologist John Rosemond says (and as Mance's parents must have known intuitively), hobbies not only keep children involved in productive activities, but they also offer other benefits: they allow children to exercise their creativity and imagination, focus their interests and talents, and learn new skills. In addition, they are educational and also help children "learn to set goals, make complex decisions, and solve all sorts of practical problems."[3] In the course of setting up the learning center and teaching the other youths to use the computers, Mance had numerous opportunities to make decisions and solve problems. As he worked to help others, he also grew personally and gained confidence in his own abilities.

The other important aspect of Mance's story is his involvement in scouting and his pursuit of the Eagle award, the highest rank of Boy Scouts of America. Few organizations have a greater commitment than the Scouts to helping youth develop good character—which is the third and most compelling reason for encouraging children's involvement in positive activities. The Boy Scout Law is itself a concise summary of good character: *A scout is trustworthy, loyal, helpful, friendly, courteous, kind, obedient, cheerful, thrifty, brave, clean, and reverent.*

Likewise, the Boy Scout Oath focuses on applying those principles in one's daily life: *On my honor, I will do my best to do my duty to God and my country, to obey the Scout law, to help other people at all times, and to keep myself physically strong, mentally awake, and morally straight.* Because scouting patrols are led by youth, with scout masters serving as mentors and coaches, there are countless opportunities for leadership, decision-making, conflict-resolution, and problem-solving. Through group activities and numerous service projects, the young men learn to put the welfare of others above their own wishes and to work together for common goals.

Other organizations such as Girl Scouts, the 4-H program (head, heart, health, and hands), the Fellowship of Christian Athletes, church youth groups, Candy Stripers (hospital youth volunteers), and school service clubs provide excellent opportunities for character growth and development. Through such groups, as well as through individual or family volunteer projects, children and teenagers learn empathy, respect, responsibility, and compassion as they serve others. They also find joy and fulfillment. For example, a thirteen-year-old hospital volunteer in my community said, "I think the thing I like most is helping people and the smiles. It gives me a feeling of happiness." Another local youth said, "It makes me happy to know I've helped people."[4]

Not only are such youth engaged in worthwhile activities, but they also have the satisfaction of knowing that they are making a difference in their communities. At the same time, they are developing the volunteer spirit which will in all likelihood carry over into their adult years. They are also associating with other youth who are equally interested in making a positive difference, thereby creating positive peer influences. Working with other youths, they develop a team spirit, and widen their circle of friends. As one young volunteer who helped build a Habitat for Humanity house observed, "We did more than build a house. We built friendships that will last a lifetime." As an added bonus of such activities, the adults leading the groups often serve as moral models and mentors for the youngsters involved, reinforcing the principles of character taught by the home, school, and church, synagogue, or mosque.

Another important way to strengthen children's character is to encourage their artistic expression. Music, dance, dramatics, and the visual arts provide excellent means of discovering and developing talent and creativity. They demand perseverance, commitment, and hard work, but at the same time these areas afford youth a wonderful sense of accomplishment when they master a difficult piece of music or learn a complicated routine. The confidence gained from performing in public also boosts self-esteem and enhances youngsters' faith in their own ability. That same confidence can in turn help them think for themselves and give them the courage to assert themselves in the face of negative peer pressure.

Early exposure to the arts adds another dimension to children's lives. Such exposure lays the foundation for a lifelong appreciation for the beauty and wonder of the world, serving as an antidote to some of the sordidness in the popular media. For example, many artists and musicians stress the emotional and spiritual benefits of art and music. Said one cellist, "My music gives me peace." Eloquently expressing the value of the arts, Wayne Dosdick reminds us that "when you give your children the gift of human handiwork, you show them how to renew their souls and fill their hearts."[5]

Like the arts, sports can also have a dramatic effect on character development. Both individual and team sports can teach lifelong character lessons *if* they are conducted within the context of fairness, honesty, respect, courtesy, and grace—in times of victory and defeat. In *The Youth Charter*, William Damon states that when players and coaches approach sports in the right way, "children learn self-discipline, persistence and cooperation. They also learn good sportsmanship: how to manage competition, how to take initiative while staying within a common set of rules, and how to balance the desire to win with the need to maintain a good relationship with opponents who also want to win." These lessons, he says, "have enduring significance for a child's later relationships and engagements."[6]

As he was dying of AIDS acquired from a tainted blood transfusion during heart surgery, Arthur Ashe wrote his memoirs, entitled *Days of Grace*. The last chapter is a poignant letter to his seven-year-old daughter, Camera. With an urgency inspired by his impending mortality, Mr. Ashe tries to compress a lifetime of concern into a few pages. Anticipating future challenges which Camera will face as she matures, he reflects on the importance of faith and family and the need to make good decisions about education, finance, and personal relationships.

In addition to fatherly counsel about a variety of other issues, Mr. Ashe advises his daughter to master at least two "life sports." (It is not surprising that a professional athlete would emphasize sports, but his reasoning has more to do with character than competition.) "Sports," he says, "are wonderful; they can bring you comfort and pleasure for the rest of your life. Sports can teach you so much about yourself, your emotions and character, how to be resolute in moments of crisis and how to fight back from the brink of defeat. In this respect, the lessons of sports cannot be duplicated easily; you quickly discover your limits but you can also build self-confidence and a positive sense of yourself."[7]

Because players typically admire and respect their coaches, it is critically important that parents and coaches reach agreement about their expectations for children's behavior on and off the athletic field. Coaches (or parents) who promote a "win at all costs" philosophy and who themselves demonstrate poor sportsmanship can do great damage. However, competition—the will to win—in and of itself is not harmful *if it is kept in proper perspective.* Former Olympic athlete and Olympic coach Brutus Hamilton captured that proper perspective when he said that "no victory is great when it is bought at the sacrifice of ideals: and no defeat is disgraceful as long as one does his best and follows the gleam of idealism."[8] That is an important lesson for children and youth to learn—both about sports and about life.

In this section, I have cited a number of activities that can keep children and teenagers constructively occupied and also have a positive influence on their character development. However, it seems appropriate to mention that while activities are important, there is also a need for balance. Children's lives should not be so structured that twelve-year-olds have to carry pocket calendars (as some do). All children and teenagers need some time to play, to daydream, and to just be kids, and they don't need or want adults hovering over them all of the time. The important point is to realize that children, especially teenagers, *are* going to find ways to fill their days. The choice is whether parents will guide them into activities which will promote positive growth and development or whether they will just let other influences rush in and fill the time vacuum.

I recall reading in a graduate course on adolescent development that during the teenage years, youth try on many faces before they find their own. In adolescence, they are attempting to discover who they are and where they fit, and they are seeking something and someone to be true to. They are also trying to make decisions about their life's work and establishing patterns concerning compassion and service to others. Involvement in a variety of positive activities such as hobbies, sports, service clubs, and youth organizations allows them to explore their interests, aptitudes, and talents. It also aids them in their search for meaning and purpose in life and helps them gain confidence as competent, capable individuals who have a contribution to make to society. Simply stated, such involvement greatly increases the likelihood that the faces our youth ultimately select as their own will reflect kindness, compassion, courage, and respect.

[1] William Glasser, *Take Effective Control of Your Life* (New York: Harper & Row, 1984), p. 195.

[2] Jim Wicker, "Computer Savvy Teen Helps Other Youths Learn," Burlington (NC) *Times News*, August 17, 1998.

[3] John Rosemond, *A Family of Value* (Kansas City: Andrews & McNeel, 1995), p. 230.

[4] Kelli Crawford, "Helping Hearts," Burlington (NC) *Times News*, August 24, 1998.

[5] Wayne Dosdick, *Golden Rules: The Ten Ethical Values Parents Need to Teach Their Children* (San Francisco, 1995), p. 110.

[6] William Damon, *The Youth Charter: How Communities Can Work Together to Raise Standards for All Our Children* (New York: The Free Press, 1997), pp. 119-120.

[7] Arthur Ashe, *Days of Grace* (New York: Alfred A. Knopf: 1993), p. 301.

[8] Russell W. Gough, *Character Is Everything: Promoting Ethical Excellence in Sports* (Fort Worth: Harcourt Brace College Publishers,1997), p. 74.

Learn to say no and mean it.

The scene is a familiar one, repeated in stores and malls all across America every day. A child spots a particular toy—perhaps one that he has seen on television—and asks for it. The mother says no. The child persists, and the mother again denies his request, reminding him that he has a roomful of toys that he rarely plays with. Intensifying his campaign, the child begs, whines, wheedles, and cries—with each plea becoming louder than the one before. Finally, out of embarrassment and frustration, the mother buys the toy. With frayed nerves, the exasperated mother leaves the store, her smiling child at her side. She knows she should have said no, but she just couldn't handle the child's public tantrum anymore.

It is easy to understand why some parents take the path of least resistance and give in to their children's requests. After all, saying yes is pleasant for everyone. The children get what they want, and the parents avoid the turmoil and embarrassment of having to deal with an emotional outburst. Yet, both common sense and developmental psychology tell us that young children must learn to deal with frustration, they must learn to delay gratification, and they must learn to respect their parents' authority if they are to become responsible adults and people of good character. Children who miss these early lessons are destined for difficulties later, especially when adolescence arrives.

Without meaning to be, many parents are overly permissive. Like the mother in the toy store, they unintentionally teach their children that if they protest long enough and loudly enough, they will get what they want or gain permission to do what they wish to do. By yielding to their children's manipulation and pressure, however, the parents are rewarding poor behavior and increasing the likelihood that similar scenes will occur again. William Kilpatrick, author of *Why Johnny Can't Tell Right from Wrong*, says that "as uncomfortable as it is for our psychological generation, parents who wish to raise well-behaved children must say no to actions that are harmful to their children." He adds that getting their way when they shouldn't is "considerably more harmful" for children than the occasional frustration of their desires.[1]

It is natural for children, and especially teenagers, to test the limits and challenge their parents. That is a part of their effort to establish their own authority and to achieve independence. However, most children and youth do not really want to be in charge; nor do they want total freedom from parental control. What many teenagers want, says Thomas Lickona, is "not freedom, but *protection*. Protection from the pressure which they feel so acutely at this stage of their moral development, to do things they really don't want to do." He adds that when parents make tough rules—even if their children put up a show of protest—they may actually be allies in the teenagers' cause.[2] That is, being able to say "My dad doesn't approve" may relieve pressure on children. By putting the onus on their parents, they are able to avoid the questionable activity and simultaneously save face with their peers.

Nevertheless, most teenagers, even those who are normally polite and respectful, will become upset at some time when a parent denies their request to do something that they *really* want to do. They may accuse their parents of being unreasonable and hopelessly out of touch and may even hurl the ultimate emotional grenade: "I hate you!" In these situations, parents need to remember that it is when children and youth are most unloving and unlovable, that they most desperately need their parents' understanding and support. Such are the times that try parents' souls and put their own character to the test. It is *very* difficult to endure the emotional upheaval and temporary rejection. However, there is comfort in knowing that most children will come to understand that their parents really do have their best interest at heart.

One way to increase the chances that youth will ultimately understand and accept their parents' decisions is to keep the lines of communication open. Having the ability and the moral courage to say no to activities that are potentially harmful to their children or others in no way implies parental stubbornness. Rather, the issue is that parents should be willing to listen to their children's point of view and be willing to negotiate on smaller matters, such as clothing or hairstyle. They should reserve their absolutely non-negotiable no's for the truly important issues affecting character and safety. In the words of someone I admire greatly, parents should be willing to bend on everything except principle.

When her daughters were teenagers, one of my friends was living in a community in which several popular girls from "good" homes became pregnant within the same school year. This was the topic of discussion at bridge clubs and in Sunday School classes. Parents were concerned that the trend might spread, so they sought some way to regain control of their youth. Several mothers decided that they would join together in an informal alliance. They agreed that the group would discuss any proposed activity (party, beach trip, etc.) and mutually decide whether the activity was appropriate and whether they would permit their children to participate. In this way, no parent would have to stand alone when saying no to their teenagers. When their children said, "but everybody else is going," they would know better.

My friend declined an invitation to be a part of the parent group. The other parents were shocked, but she stood firm. Her reason? "I wanted to retain control of my own children. I knew that some of the parents had more liberal attitudes toward such things as teen-aged drinking, and I was concerned that the group might agree on an activity that I could not support. I had never had a problem saying no when I believed it was in the best interest of my children, and I didn't want to feel pressured by other parents to go along with something that I thought was inappropriate." Recently, her grown daughter told her how much she respected her mother's stand and the fact that she never hesitated to say no. "I didn't always agree with you," her daughter said, "but I always respected you."

One of the great concerns about teenagers is the potential harm that lies in peer influence. We want them to have the courage to take a moral stand—and to stand alone if necessary. By resisting her own form of peer pressure, this mother provided a powerful model for her children. She clearly established her authority as a parent and took responsibility for her own children. In the process, she made a valuable contribution to her children's character development and bequeathed to them what William Damon calls "the single most important moral legacy that comes out of the parent-child relationship"—respect for their parents' authority.[3]

I greatly admired author and humorist Erma Bombeck. She had a special knack for making us laugh at ourselves and also had a rare talent for helping us sense the eternal in the ordinary business of life. The following column, which she wrote in 1976, touches on the major principles of character development, and it serves as a poignant reminder of the love that prompts parents to say no, even when it hurts. It is, I believe, an appropriate summary of this chapter.

MOTHER'S LOVE IS FAR STRONGER THAN CHILDREN'S ANGER

"You don't love me!"

How many times have your kids laid that one on you?

How many times have you, as a parent, resisted the urge to tell them how much?

Someday, when my children are old enough to understand the logic that motivates a mother, I will tell them.

I loved you enough to bug you about where you were going, with whom and what time to get home.

I loved you enough to insist you buy a bike that you could afford with your own money.

I loved you enough to be silent and let you discover your friend was a creep.

I loved you enough to make you return a Milky Way with a bite out of it to a drugstore and confess, "I stole this."

I loved you enough to stand over you for two hours while you cleaned your bedroom, a job that would have taken me 15 minutes.

I loved you enough to say, "Yes, you can go to Disney World on Mother's Day."

I loved you enough to let you see anger, disappointment, disgust, and tears in my eyes.

I loved you enough not to make excuses for your lack of respect or your bad manners.

I loved you enough to admit that I was wrong and ask your forgiveness.

I loved you enough to ignore what every other mother did or said.

I loved you enough to let you assume the responsibility for your own actions at age 6, 10, or 16.

I loved you enough to figure you would lie about the party being chaperoned, but forgave you for it—after discovering I was right.

I loved you enough to accept you for what you are, not what I wanted you to be.

But most of all, I loved you enough to say no when you hated me for it. That was the hardest part of all.[4]

[1] William Kilpatrick, *Why Johnny Can't Tell Right from Wrong* (New York: Simon & Schuster, 1992), p. 257.

[2] Thomas Lickona, *Raising Good Children* (New York: Bantam Books, 1994), p. 397.

[3] William Damon, *The Moral Child* (New York: The Free Press, 1988), p. 52.

[4] Erma Bombeck, "Mother's Love is Far Stronger than Children's Anger," reprinted with permission of The Aaron M. Priest Literary Agency, Inc., 708 Third Avenue, 23rd floor, New York, NY 10017-4103.

Know where your children are, what they are doing, and with whom.

In 1996, Laurence Steinberg, a psychology professor at Temple University, reported on the most extensive study ever conducted on the forces affecting teenagers' interest and performance in school. Over a ten-year period, his research team surveyed 20,000 young people and their parents in communities across America. It is not surprising that Dr. Steinberg and his colleagues found that the most successful students were those whose parents were involved with school activities and made education the top priority in the home. What is surprising and disappointing, however, is that *only one-third of the students said that they have a daily conversation with their parents*, and forty percent indicated that their parents *never* attend any of their school programs or activities. Even more startling is the fact that *half of the parents admitted that they do not know who their children's friends are or how their children spend their free time*.[1]

Children today are more sophisticated than previous generations were. Kindergartners use computers with an ease which many adults envy. Some elementary school children regularly board airplanes alone for cross-country flights for parental visits mandated by custody agreements. Through the media—and sometimes through personal experience—they have seen war and violence up close. Even young children exhibit an astonishing awareness of sex, casually using terms that some of their parents didn't know until they were in high school. They also mature physically at earlier ages than before.

Because children and youth today look and sound mature, we occasionally forget that they are still children. Despite outward appearances, children and teenagers are not developmentally ready to handle some of the situations in which they find themselves. However, it sometimes takes a serious incident to remind us that even smart, good kids need strong support, supervision, and structure from their parents. As the following incident illustrates, parents cannot merely *assume* that their children will always make good decisions and use good judgment.

Jill (not her real name) was from a "good" home. Her well-educated parents were prosperous and provided for her education in a private high school. She had generally been an obedient and responsible youth. Her mother knew that Jill and her friends sometimes drank at parties, even though she had tried to discourage it. Nevertheless, Jill's parents trusted her and were shocked when the sixteen-year-old missed her 1:00 a.m. curfew one Friday night. Their efforts to reach her by pager and by telephone were unsuccessful.

When the phone finally rang at 3:00 a.m., the mother answered with some apprehension, hoping to hear Jill's voice. However, it wasn't her daughter. Instead, it was a police officer informing her that he had arrested Jill for driving while intoxicated. She did not have her driver's license with her, she couldn't walk a straight line, and she also had an empty wine bottle on the back seat. Because her blood-alcohol level was so high, Jill would be required to spend the weekend in a juvenile detention center.

How did Jill get into this situation? She went out with her friend Ann. The two of them then went to a party at the home of a boy whose parents were out of town for the weekend. According to Jill, "everyone" was there, and many of the teenagers—including Jill—were consuming large amounts of alcohol, celebrating one last "bash" before the new school term began. Because she had drunk so much ("I was drunk, but not as drunk as the other kids were"), Jill didn't even realize she had missed her curfew. After a friend made a scene at the party, Jill decided to leave in Ann's car and drive to Ann's home, where she would spend the night. (Ann wanted to remain at the party and planned to get someone else to give her a ride home.) Some of the other youths, who had apparently enjoyed their own private party in Ann's car, were responsible for leaving the wine bottle there.

At her hearing, Jill and her parents regarded themselves as different from the other teenagers and their parents that they encountered in court, feeling that they didn't belong there. Nevertheless, they had to face the fact that Jill was a drunk driver and that she had committed a serious crime—and that they did indeed belong there. They also had to acknowledge that Jill had been lying about her secret drinking problem. (The reality that she could have been killed—or could have killed someone else—had already hit them.)

Reflecting on the incident, Jill's mother said that they were really very lucky that the incident happened because it jarred them out of complacency. She added, "Because Jill is a take-charge kind of girl—verbal and funny and smart—it's sometimes easy to forget that she's still a child. But nothing should have clouded that fact that, at sixteen, she had only a sixteen-year-old's untested judgment. I now know I can't just sit back and let her figure everything out for herself. She's not an adult yet—even if she is six inches taller than I am."[2]

This experience of Jill and her parents illustrates the importance of parents' knowing where their children are, whom they are with, and what they are doing. That task is much easier when children are small. As they experience increasing independence, it is more difficult—but no less important—to monitor their activities. Does this mean that parents should maintain such rigid control that children cannot have a good time or spend time with their friends? Of course not, but it does mean that parents should provide some clear guidance as to which behaviors are acceptable and which are not. It also means that parents should get to know their children's friends (and their parents) and should be aware of where and how their children are spending their time and money.

For children to mature, they need opportunities to interact not only with adults, but with their peers as well. From their parents and other adults, they learn values, habits, and skills that help prepare them to become responsible family members and good citizens.[3] Through their equally important friendships with peers, they learn "cooperation and mutual respect, the rules of friendship, and the importance of fair play." They also learn to open up to others and to share confidences, self-doubts, and insecurities—all of which are necessary for mental health and well-being.[4]

Despite the many benefits of peer relations, however, they are also fraught with dangers. While these dangers vary, the most common risks involve substance abuse, binge drinking, and sex. (According to Dr. William Damon, sex has become for many young people "a kind of Russian roulette—a sport for thrills that flirts with disastrous consequences such as AIDS or other life-changing ones such as early pregnancy.[5]) Because the peer culture has such a powerful influence on our youth, it just makes sense to attempt to understand it and to try to channel that influence in positive directions. Parents can do that only if they are actively engaged and meaningfully involved in their children's lives.

Military hero Colin Powell devotes much of his time and energy to an organization called America's Promise. That organization is trying to develop and coordinate a volunteer effort to rescue what he calls "the lost children"—children who are growing up on the streets. These are children who have poor self-esteem and limited language skills, who know nothing about shame or guilt, and whose lives are without purpose, structure, or discipline. According to General Powell, there is nobody, no adult family member who is involved in their lives, encouraging them and trying to teach them right from wrong. As a result, the street takes over. Such children are victims of extreme parental disengagement.

In contrast to the youths he is trying to help, General Powell grew up in a world in which parents closely monitored their children's behavior and whereabouts. Both of his parents worked, but they were part of an extensive network of friends and family members who looked after each other's children. Colin's sister Marilyn once remarked that when her brother "walked down the block, a pair of eyes followed him from behind every curtain."[6] If the young Powell was somewhere he shouldn't be or doing something he shouldn't be doing, his parents were sure to find out. The news of any inappropriate conduct was likely to reach home before he did.

Of his own youth, General Powell says, "The communities were together. Families, parents were together. There was a church that was an important presence, or a synagogue. I sometimes compare it to a pinball machine: You had flippers which constantly kept the kid in place."[7] Unfortunately, communities such as the one in which General Powell grew up are now rare. Like the elder Powells, most of today's parents work and cannot directly monitor their children's activities as closely as they want and need to. Unlike the Powells, however, they don't have the extended family or neighborhood support which was common a generation ago.

Clearly, most current communities—and their churches, families, and neighbors—do not serve as "flippers" to keep the kids in place. Consequently, some parents are forming alliances with other parents and community members to protect children and youth from some of the negative influences in today's society. One such organization is Parents Who Care (PWC), which was founded in Palo Alto, California, by a mother who was shocked to learn that her teenage daughter was being pressured by her friends to drink alcohol and smoke pot. More than 500 parents became involved in a community effort to attack the social acceptance of alcohol and drug use among the youth and to establish a more positive atmosphere for the teenagers—to "create the kind of atmosphere where the 'norm' for teenagers is to develop their talents to the fullest."[8]

Parents Who Care agreed on a set of guidelines for parents who wanted to gain better control and provide a more wholesome atmosphere for their teenagers. Interestingly, their actions did not lead to a youthful revolt. Instead, parents found that there was less arguing about rules and better cooperation from their teenagers. The youths realized that their parents cared about them and were trying to respond to a threatening situation. In all probability, the children felt a sense of relief and security by having their parents exert more control. Following is a summary of the list developed by PWC:

Except for attending school or community events, teenagers will stay home on school nights. (There will be no more "running the streets or driving around aimlessly looking for fun.")

All youth will have a weekend curfew, with older teenagers being allowed to stay out later than their younger counterparts. (PWC established a different curfew for each grade level, nine through twelve.)

Parents are to feel free to call host parents when their child is invited to a party to make sure that there will be adequate adult supervision and that drugs and alcohol will not be allowed.

Parents are to be visible at their own children's parties. Any youths who do not behave appropriately or who have drugs or alcohol should be asked to leave and their parents called. Also, to prevent the introduction of drugs and alcohol, young guests who leave the party should not be allowed to return.

When children or teenagers go out, they need to leave telephone numbers where their parents can reach them. (Although it was not part of the PWC list, parents should afford their children the same courtesy.)

Parents are to assure dating teenagers that they will provide transportation any time if they need it.

Parents should be awake when their youngsters come home.

Parents should get to know their children's friends and their parents.[9]

Another parent group is Safe Homes (P. O. Box 702, Livingston, NJ 07039). This national organization "encourages parents to sign a contract stipulating that when parties are held in one another's homes they will adhere to strict no-alcohol/no-drug-use rule."[10] Participants make the following pledge:

I will not serve nor will I allow anyone under the legal drinking age to consume alcohol in my home or on my property.

I will not allow the use of illegal drugs in my home or on my property.

I will not allow parties or gatherings in my home without proper adult supervision.[11]

The Youth Charter is another, more extensive group approach to promoting positive, wholesome activities for adolescents, and it involves the entire community, including the youth. In developing a youth charter, parents and others who are in a position to influence young people sit down together and discuss their fears, their hopes, and their dreams for the youngsters in the community. Then they draw up a charter which "calls young people to higher standards of behavior in four areas—spirituality, sportsmanship, youth activities, and alcohol and drug abuse—but also urges adults to give clear direction."[12] William Damon, who has worked with communities across America in drawing up their own youth charters, says that "a clear, united stand about what is acceptable behavior goes a long way toward countering the mixed message young people get from music, TV, movies—and often, from adults."[13]

Such formal parent groups can be helpful in addressing major character issues, setting expectations, and communicating those expectations to the youth of the community. They enable parents to present a united front on overall guiding principles—on the character issues—related to activities for youth. In contrast to the informal alliance mentioned in Strategy Seventeen (Learn How to Say No), they do not involve "voting" on whether parents should grant permission for their children to attend particular functions. These decisions are—and should be—the prerogative of individual parents. In no way do parent participants relinquish their right or their responsibility to act in the best interest of their own children.

Even in the absence of organizations such as Parents Who Care or Safe Homes, parents need to keep informed about what is happening in their community, especially among children and youth. Recognizing that, many parents take advantage of their own informal networks. When their children are invited to social events, for example, they call the host parents and ask questions about such things as whether the parents will be home and visible during the party and whether drinking and drugs will be prohibited. They attend school functions and volunteer to chaperone youth events, getting to know their children's friends and their parents. They also maintain close contact with their children's teachers, requesting reports of any changes in attitudes, behavior, or academic performance. Most important, they keep the lines of communication open with their own children. They are, in contrast to half of the parents in Dr. Steinberg's study, actively engaged and meaningfully involved in their children's lives.

In the 1980s, when President Reagan was involved in international negotiations for nuclear disarmament, his slogan was "trust and verify." The implication was that we should expect the best intentions from others, but as a matter of prudence, we should also verify that they were indeed honoring their commitments. As parents attempt to shepherd youngsters through childhood and adolescence, Mr. Reagan's slogan seems to apply. Adults need to communicate in countless ways that we care about children and that we expect the best from them, but that we also take seriously our responsibility to establish standards and to monitor, chaperone, and supervise. To do less is to take reckless chances with our children's future.

. . . .

[1] Laurence Steinberg, *Beyond the Classroom: Why School Reform Has Failed and What Parents Need to Do (New York: Simon & Schuster, 1996), p. 130.*

[2] Melanie Franklin (name changed for privacy) and Jean Gonick, "My Daughter Was a Drunk Driver," *Good Housekeeping*, August, 1998, pp. 88-92.

[3] William Damon, *The Youth Charter: How Communities Can Work Together to Raise Standards for All Our Children* (New York: The Free Press, 1997), p. 126.

[4] Ibid.

[5] Ibid., p. 129.

[6] Cokie Roberts and Steven V. Roberts, "Colin Powell: Striking a Nerve," *USA Weekend*, November 14-16, 1997, p. 5.

[7] Ibid.

[8] Jeane Westin, *The Coming Parent Revolution* (New York: Bantam Books, 1981), ˈp. 245.

[9] Ibid., pp. 245-246.

[10] *Growing up Drug Free: A Parent's Guide to Prevention* (Washington, DC: U. S. Department of Education, undated), p. 45.

[11] Thomas Lickona, *Educating for Character: How Our Schools Can Teach Respect and Responsibility* (New York: Bantam Books, 1992), p. 391.

[12] Reed Karaim, "Can a Town Agree on What's Best for Teens?" *USA Weekend*, November 14-16, 1998, p. 16.

[13] Ibid.

Don't cover for your children or make excuses for their inappropriate behavior.

One of my responsibilities as a school administrator was to handle all of the parent complaints coming to the superintendent's office. I also chaired the system-wide appeals committee for suspensions and expulsions for a number of years. Although the vast majority of parents were reasonable and were supportive of efforts to help their children develop responsible behavior, I occasionally encountered adults who seemed more concerned about ensuring that their children escaped the consequences of their behavior than about helping them learn from their mistakes.

They covered for their children when they were dishonest; they made excuses when their children failed to meet their commitments; and even in the face of irrefutable evidence of their children's misconduct, they tried to deflect blame to others. When their children were disciplined, for example, their distress was not directed at their sons or daughters for skipping school, being disrespectful to their teachers, violating the drug policy, fighting, or cheating on exams. Instead, they berated school personnel, looking for legal loopholes and threatening to sue *somebody* if their children were not completely exonerated.

The real issue for such parents—and their counterparts in school systems across America—was not their children's character. Rather, it was the avoidance of any family embarrassment or inconvenience and any smudge on the student's record. In rare cases, some parents even resorted to a show of force—attempting to intimidate school personnel into backing down from enforcing policy where *their* children were concerned. When such situations occurred, I always felt great concern for the children and the character lessons their parents were teaching them.

In our society, it seems that almost everyone can find a legal escape hatch or can claim victim status on some level. In government, in sports, and in the entertainment world, examples abound of people who have connived and lied about wrongdoing. How often have we—and our youth—watched as some famous person has looked straight into the television camera and denied guilt, only to have a very different set of facts emerge later. Euphemisms like "I misspoke myself" and "mistakes were made" have become part of our national vocabulary. Recent events have even communicated the cynical message that you can literally get away with murder if you can afford the right lawyers or if you can present yourself as a victim of circumstances.

Baltimore Sun columnist Linell Smith says that it seems as if celebrities have "made an art form of shrugging off responsibility." As examples, he cites the following: Baseball's Darryl Strawberry, who "blamed his alcoholism and drug addiction on the demands of being a celebrity"; Erik and Lyle Menendez, who claimed to have been abused by their parents and were not, therefore, guilty of murdering them; and tennis pro Jennifer Capriati, whose father took the blame for her arrest for possessing marijuana, stating that he had pressured her too hard to compete when she was young. These days, Mr. Smith maintains, "It seems as if bad behavior is not so much explained as it is excused."[1]

Parents naturally love their children and want to protect them from pain and harm. Unfortunately, some carry that protective urge to extremes, practicing what John Rosemond calls "parenting by helicopter." That is, they hover over their children, trying to remove every obstacle to their happiness, comfort, and safety—even if their children are in the wrong. Such shielding of children and youth from the logical consequences of their own misconduct and errors in judgment is dangerous, however, because it fails to teach them personal responsibility. Even more serious is the fact that it undermines social customs and law by communicating to children and youth that they are somehow exempt from the regulations that govern others' behavior. Ultimately, it fosters what Stephen Covey calls "spoiled, law-unto-self behavior."[2]

To illustrate, consider the following incident that occurred in Chicago; it is an extreme example of a parent's blatant efforts to excuse a child's criminal activity. A trucker traveling on the Kennedy Expressway was startled by the loud thud of a huge rock crashing onto his hood. As soon as he could safely pull off the road, he examined the damage to this truck. Then, looking toward a restraining wall, he saw two young boys who were throwing rocks onto the expressway. The driver chased them on foot and managed to catch one of them, grabbing him by the arm. After getting the youth's name and address, he let him go.

The truck driver immediately reported the incident to the police. As the police officer was taking down the details from the victim, an obviously angry adult male approached them, with the thirteen-year-old boy in tow. Anticipating a profound apology, both the driver and the officer were astounded at what happened next. The boy's father immediately launched a verbal assault on the driver, threatening to sue him for grabbing his son's arm. The shocked police officer—to whom the boy admitted having thrown the rock—explained to the man that not only had his son caused extensive and expensive damage to the truck, but he could have killed the driver or his passenger if the rock had hit the windshield instead of the hood.

How did the father respond? Continuing to defend his son, he said, "That's not the point. The point is that when he grabbed my son, he hurt his arm. So I'm going to sue." Once again, the officer tried to reason with the father, emphasizing that *his son had admitted throwing the rocks*. Adamantly refusing to acknowledge the severity of his son's actions *or* his confession of the crime, the father said, "Well, my son didn't know what he was doing. He's an innocent victim, and he says he didn't do it. Besides, nobody read him his rights."[3]

James Stenson has observed that children develop character by what they see, by what they hear, and by what they are repeatedly led to do. The child in Chicago saw and heard a very negative message about respect, responsibility, and good citizenship. His father clearly did not understand that when children or teenagers break the rules—whether in the home, at school, or in the larger community—they need to learn to take responsibility for their actions and to accept the consequences. Although adults may be tempted to protect them, it is a disservice to rescue them. Parents can love, support, and understand when their children make mistakes, but they should make it very clear that they do not and will not condone or excuse poor behavior. In the short run, it might seem attractive to rush in and become a temporary hero by rescuing them, but the wise parent understands that such intervention actually short-circuits their children's future responsibility and maturity.

Psychologist John Rosemond advises parents to practice "The Agony Principle." That is, they "should not agonize over anything the child is doing or failing to do if the child is perfectly capable of agonizing over it himself."[4] When parents take on the emotional and other consequences of a child's misbehavior, they unwittingly accept responsibility for that misconduct. In essence, they take ownership of the problem, relieving the child of any responsibility or guilt. If children are to develop a conscience and strong moral character, they need to experience feelings of regret and remorse when they behave badly. In other words, they *need* to feel bad and to take steps to make amends when their conduct violates the rules or hurts others.[5]

To illustrate the latter point, reflect for a moment on your own moral journey from childhood to adulthood. What were the events from which you learned the most? For many of us, they were the times when our parents refused to extricate us from the consequences of our own misconduct or poor judgment. Perhaps it was a time when you received a speeding ticket, and your father quietly informed you that you would need to earn money to pay the fine, and the resulting increase in insurance premiums on the family car. Maybe it was when you were a small child and stole a package of gum and your mother marched you back into the store and insisted that you tell the manager what you had done, apologize, and explain what you had learned from the incident. Or was it the year when you decided that basketball was more important than junior English and your parents informed you that *you*—not they—would pay for the summer school make-up and that your scheduled beach trip would be canceled because you would need to study. Could it have been the time when you and several friends engaged in what you considered harmless vandalism at your school and were arrested—and your parents let you spend the night in jail?

Although actions such as these may have been difficult or embarrassing for your parents, they understood that the long-term effects on your character were worth the temporary inconvenience. Even though they—like most parents—sometimes tempered justice with mercy, they made sure that you learned from your poor judgment.

Obviously, refusing to excuse inappropriate behavior does not have to be a harsh assertion of parental authority. When children break the rules or violate the laws of society, it is important for parents to let them know that they do not approve of or condone their inappropriate or illegal actions. They need to talk with the youngesters about the choices they made and the consequences of those choices—for themselves and for others. They also need to help their children learn from their mistakes by helping them reflect on what they did and how the youths might handle similar situations in the future. However, this can and should be done within the context of love and support.

Regardless of the situation, it is important for parents to assure their children of their love. At the same time, they need to communicate clearly that parental love does *not* absolve their children and teenagers of responsibility for their actions. All parents need to remember that loving your children doesn't require you to shield and protect them from the results of their poor decisions. It does, however, require that you be there to offer support and encouragement as they learn from their mistakes.[6]

[1] Linell Smith, "Is Anyone to Blame for Anything Anymore?" *The Baltimore Sun*, reprinted in *The Greensboro (NC) News and Record*, August 21, 1994.

[2] Stephen Covey, *Principle-Centered Leadership* (New York: Simon & Schuster, 1992), pp. 126-127.

[3] Mike Royko, "Another Innocent Victim," *Reader's Digest*, February, 1995, pp. 83-84.

[4] John Rosemond, *A Family of Value* (Kansas City: Andrews & McNeel, 1995), p. 185.

[5] John Rosemond, *Six-Point Plan for Raising Happy, Healthy Children* (Kansas City: Andrews & McNeel, 1997), p. 99.

[6] Thomas Knowles and W. R. Spence, *Parenting Teens: Straight Talk* (Waco, TX: WRS Group, 1993). p. 3.

Know what TV shows, videos, and movies your children are watching.

I t was like a dream, and then I woke up." These were the words of Michael Carneal after he shot into a gathering of students who were holding an informal prayer meeting at their high school in West Paducah, Kentucky. The fourteen-year-old had hinted to some of his friends for almost a year that he might take control of the school and shoot some students. Yet no one took the youth's comments seriously, and no one was prepared for the tragedy that ensued. When the shooting ended, three students were dead, and five more were wounded, one of whom was paralyzed.

The police were as stunned as everyone else at the senseless slaughter. Seeking to understand his motive, they asked Michael whether he had ever seen anything like the killing before. At that point, the youth replied that he had "seen this done" in *Basketball Diaries*. What is the plot of that movie? The main character has a dream about breaking down a door in school and systematically slaying several students while other classmates cheer. Then he aims the gun at his teacher, whom he has cornered behind a desk. The youth wakes up as he pulls the trigger.[1]

America has long suspected that violence in the media contributes to violence in real life. In recent months and years, we have been repeatedly shocked by reports of vicious, senseless assaults by youngsters. When we ask why, the answer often comes back—at least in part—to what we are allowing our children to watch and listen to. Warnings about the effects of repeated exposure to violence in the movies, television, and music are not new, but they have largely gone unheeded by too many adults. In 1974, for example, Fredric Wertham sounded the following alarm in "School for Violence, Mayhem, and the Mass Media":

> If someone had said a generation ago that a school to teach the art and uses of violence would be established, no one would have believed him. He would have been told that those whose mandate is the mental welfare of children, the parents and the professionals, would prevent it. And yet this education for violence is precisely what has happened and is still happening; we teach violence to young people to an extent that has never been known before in history.[2]

When he wrote the article, Dr. Wertham was a practicing psychiatrist evaluating and treating individuals—many of them juveniles—who had committed violent acts. From many personal encounters and his research, he was absolutely convinced that children not only learn violent behavior from the media, but that they also learn to associate violence with that which is good and just.

Despite Dr. Wertham's work and that of many other professionals in medicine, psychology, and education, we continue to get lost in the debate as to whether viewing violence leads to violent behavior. In the meantime, our children go on killing and being killed. That the debate continues is particularly amazing because since 1955 there have been more than 1,000 studies, reports, and commentaries on the effects of television violence.[3] One of the leading experts on the subject, Dr. Leonard Eron, summarizes the massive amount of research by saying that "*there can no longer be any doubt that heavy exposure to televised violence is one of the causes of aggressive behavior, crime, and violence in society. The evidence comes from both the laboratory and real-life studies. Television violence affects youngsters of all ages, of both genders, at all socioeconomic levels, and all levels of intelligence.*"[4] The research has focused primarily on television, but there is no reason to believe that violence on the movie screen differs in its effects from that on the television screen. Of equal concern are the video games that teach children to obliterate their "enemies" and the heavy metal music and "gangsta" rap which resonate with a raucous beat of violence, hatred, and hostility.

How are children affected by all of this violence? Obviously, not all who watch violent programming will go out and rape or kill, but the evidence clearly shows that children who watch a lot of violent programming are more likely to be aggressive in their play and in their interactions with others. They are also more likely to settle their conflicts with hostile physical or verbal attacks instead of seeking peaceful resolutions. In other words, they emulate the violent heroes they have seen and heard. Because violence in the media is often associated with strong, attractive figures who experience no punishment for their actions, youngsters have little reason to doubt the rightness of their own conduct.

It is particularly disturbing that some of the most violent programs of all are those targeted at children and teenagers. For example, the Center for Media and Public Affairs conducted an eighteen-hour (one full broadcast day) study of ten stations in the Washington, D. C. area and found that the 144 videotapes shown on MTV during that time period contained as much violence as all three of the major commercial television networks (ABC, NBC, and CBS) combined. That the average number of violent acts for all stations was 100 per hour was alarming, but the most shocking surprise was that *the cartoons contained by far the highest number of incidents of violence of any programs.* The effects of this violence are especially harmful for preschool children, who have not yet developed the ability to distinguish fantasy from reality.[5]

Another effect of extensive exposure to media violence is that children and youth may become numb to the very real effects of violence on others. In a sense, they are inoculated against the compassion that human beings normally feel for one another, and they lose the awareness that bullets kill, slapping and punching hurt, and sexual attacks are physically and emotionally devastating. The result is that some youths can callously witness violence to others and feel nothing. I encountered this attitude firsthand when a high school student told a disciplinary hearing panel I was chairing that if he witnessed a brutal beating of another teenager, he would offer assistance or seek help *only* if the victim were his friend. Otherwise, he said, it wouldn't bother him at all.

It is one thing to read that violence has such an effect. It is quite another to hear a young person proudly espouse such beliefs. I agree with William Damon that this desensitization is one of the most alarming outcomes of media violence because it breaks down the "natural barrier of empathy that normally makes the thought of harming another person repulsive."[6] Another major concern is that media violence is often presented in a comical way—especially in cartoons and programs designed for children. Through pratfalls and buffoonery, youngsters learn to laugh at the injury and discomfort inflicted on others. These are hardly the lessons we want children to learn about respect, kindness, and caring.

Furthermore, because violence in the movies and on television is depicted with such graphic detail and realism, viewers—especially young children—may become frightened and traumatized by what they see. In fact, otherwise well-adjusted individuals of any age can experience the "mean world syndrome." That is, they start to believe that the world is a hostile, dangerous place, and they live in fear and dread that they too will be victims of a violent assault. (A poignant example of this occurred in my community several years ago when a four-year-old attempted to get on a bus while carrying a butcher knife. He said that he needed it "for protection.")

Even if scientific opinion did not support the link between viewing violence in the media and real-life behavior, common sense would tell us that children should not be exposed to a steady diet of murder, rape, and assault. Wayne Dosdick cuts through all the debate and gets to the very heart of the matter by stating that "sociologists can argue forever whether watching television leads to violent behavior. If it does, then surely it should not be watched. But even if it does not, it endorses—even if passively—an attitude and an atmosphere that disregards the sanctity of human life and the preciousness of human relationships."[7]

Despite its potential to harm our youth and our society, however, violence is by no means the only reason for adults to monitor and take responsibility for what children watch on television and in the movies. Beyond the gratuitous violence, the media are communicating some powerful moral messages which are not consistent with the beliefs of most families. In fact, a national poll showed that the majority of Americans consider television to be hostile to their own moral and spiritual values.[8] Mortimer Zuckerman, editor-in-chief of *U. S. News & World Report*, speaks for many thoughtful adults when he asserts that "TV and music often seem to honor everything the true American ethic abhors—violence, infidelity, drugs, drinking—and to despise everything that it embraces—religion, marriage, respect for authority."[9]

In a similar vein, Michael Medved, movie critic and author of *Hollywood vs. America,* urges parents to pay attention to what their children are watching and listening to. He says that "on many of the important issues in contemporary life, popular entertainment seems to go out of its way to challenge conventional notions of decency." Mr. Medved adds, "Nearly all parents want to convey to their children the importance of self-discipline, hard work, and decent manners; but the entertainment media celebrate vulgar behavior, contempt for all authority, and obscene language."[10] Because of the constant repetition of these messages, television and the other media can and often do lead children to believe that such conduct and language are both normal and acceptable.

Of particular concern are the images of family life and sex that are presented in the media. Television programs of the 1950s and 1960s, such as *Father Knows Best, Ozzie and Harriet,* and *Leave It to Beaver* portrayed parents as honest and caring people who were very capable of leading and guiding their children. The children might engage in immature activities or even occasionally test the limits on obedience, but typically they were respectful of their parents. Families could watch the programs together without fear of embarrassment—either from the programs *or* the commercials. Also, real-life parents frequently found their own values reinforced as the plots unfolded.

In contrast, today's programs not only do not complement the moral messages parents are trying to communicate to their children, but they often directly contradict and undermine those messages. On situation comedies, talk shows, and other television programs, parents have become an easy target for satire and ridicule. In fact, parent-bashing appears to be very much in vogue. Rather than respectable, worthy individuals, they are portrayed as irresponsible, cruel, stupid, or all of the above. In TV-land it is often the children who are the problem-solvers and who serve as a source of guidance and counsel to their clueless parents.

From sarcastic, wisecracking youth such as Beavis, Butthead, and Bart Simpson, children learn to be disrespectful toward their parents and to be irreverent and cynical about life in general. For example, one early episode of *The Simpsons* showed the family saying grace before a meal. What was the blessing? "God, we paid for all this food ourselves, so thanks for nothing." Such are the youthful role models our children see on television. Rather than inspiring the young to be better and more noble, the media seem to highlight human nature at its worst. It really does seem, as the authors of *The War Against Parents* say it so well, that the entertainment industry not only seriously undercuts parents, but is "hell-bent on destroying the values they stand for."[11]

Since the deregulation of television during the 1980s, the limits of decency have been pushed back further and further. In no area is this more obvious than in the portrayal of sex. Television programs in prime time are filled with sexual references and jokes. Most of the sexual encounters are presented outside the context of marriage. The result is that one of the most precious of human relationships is debased and trivialized, and children and adolescents gain a very distorted view of love, courtship, and marriage. Through countless messages, some subtle and some shouted, our youth learn that "sex should be viewed as an end in itself, a glorious form of recreation that has nothing to do with responsibility or commitment."[12]

In many ways, television has become the principal transmitter of values to our children, even though they are not the values which most of us want them to learn. How has this happened? Simply because the majority of American youngsters spend far more time watching television than conversing with their parents. Because the television set is almost always on in many homes, its messages blend into a subtle kind of background music. Without being consciously aware of its impact, some parents have allowed television to replace them (and schools and churches) as the major moral influences in their children's lives.

According to figures from the Center for Media Literacy, the television set in a typical home is on an average of more than seven hours a day, or approximately fifty hours a week (compared with about thirty hours children spend in school each week).[13] By the time they enter kindergarten, most children will have watched television for about 4,000 hours, enough time to complete a four-year degree. At the end of their elementary school years, those same children will have seen 8,000 murders and witnessed 100,000 acts of violence on television.[14] These statistics are especially important in that during children's most vulnerable years—the years in which their values are formed and their conscience developed—it is television which is having the greatest impact on their attitudes and behavior.

So pervasive is television's influence that some children actually prefer watching television over interacting with their families. An incident that occurred on *Bill Moyers' Journal* several years ago illustrates this point. The interviewer posed this dilemma to a group of elementary school children: Suppose you had to give up one of the following for the rest of your life—watching television or talking to your father. Which would you choose? Sadly, *almost half said they would rather give up talking to their father!*[15] Surely, it is not an overstatement to say that the media—especially television—is a "teacher that competes with all of us for the hearts and minds of children."[16]

Clearly, the media can have a strong, negative impact on the character of our children and youth. The question is, what can parents do to offset the lessons they are learning from television and the movies? One drastic approach is to get rid of the television set altogether, but for most of us, that is not a practical option. Short of that, however, parents can help their families become more responsible consumers of the media. The first step in that direction is to monitor the programs family members are watching. Keeping a log of viewing for a week can be very enlightening to both parents and children. All will probably be amazed at the amount of time they are spending in front of the TV.

Parents can also involve their children (as appropriate for their ages) in critiquing and discussing the programs they watch, using questions such as the following: What are the lessons children learn from the programs? Are the messages consistent with our family's values? Does the laughter or sound track teach that coarse language and rude behavior are good and worthy of imitation? What are the messages about violence, family life, sex, drugs and alcohol, good manners, honesty, or responsibility? How did the characters' actions help or hurt others? Which of the actions were real and which were special effects?

Ironic though it seems, parents need to make time to watch television with their children and talk about what they are seeing. Whether it is the news, a documentary, or an entertainment program, there will likely be some excellent teachable moments. Parents need to make their views known when something occurs that violates the family's values and help their children think through why the action on the screen was inappropriate or morally wrong. This parental involvement and guidance is especially important where violence is concerned. Research tells us that children are at much greater risk of imitating the violence they see in the media if their parents either seem to condone it or simply leave a "violence vacuum" by saying nothing about their own beliefs.[17]

Another step to protect children from the negative influence of the media and help them become more discriminating viewers is to limit the amount of television the family watches. One worthwhile strategy is to develop a schedule based on carefully selected programs rather than allowing children to automatically turn on the set to see what is on.

Implementing the plan might be a challenge at first, but the end results make the effort worthwhile. For example, consider the experience of Jim Trelease, author of *The New Read-Aloud Handbook*.

He and his wife decided that they would no longer allow their two children to watch television on school nights. The children, a kindergarten son and a fourth-grade daughter, cried every night for four months following that decision, and the parents not only experienced resistance from their children, but they were also subjected to an unanticipated amount of pressure from their own peers.

After the initial adjustment, however, the Treleases began to see some very positive effects on their family. Suddenly, they had time to read together as a family, play board games, bake cookies, play on church sports teams, and develop long-neglected hobbies. The children were able to complete their homework without rushing through it, and they did their chores with less conflict than before. Best of all, Mr. Trelease says, the family found time to talk—really talk and listen—to one another. Having reduced the amount of time spent passively in front of the TV, the parents saw their children's imaginations come back to life, and they rediscovered the joy of truly meaningful, positive family interactions.

In time, they modified the schedule to allow each child to watch one school night show per week, subject to the parents' approval and after homework and chores were completed. By limiting them to only one show during the week, the parents taught the children to be discriminating in their choices and to distinguish worthwhile programming from trash TV. The result was that "they became very choosy, refusing to waste the privilege, and began using a critical eye in evaluating shows."[18] In short, the parents took an active role in controlling their children's viewing habits, reducing their exposure to harmful influences. Simultaneously, they taught them to be better, more selective consumers of the media.

Other families are discovering the benefits of turning off the television set, even if only for one week each year. National TV Turn-Off Week, which is observed in April of each year, was initiated in 1995. The project has spread to 50,000 schools across the country, and in 1997, more than four million Americans participated. Although many of the children—and some of their parents—resisted the idea at first, the majority who gave up television for a week were glad that they did. One eight-year-old said, for example, "It was sort of boring at first [but] we played outside more than usual. And I read more than five books that week."[19]

Similarly, a third-grader who participated in an earlier TV Turn-Off, stated that "it was kind of fun without the TV. It helped me get closer to my family." A single mother working two jobs remarked, "I hadn't realized that I was losing ground with my children. This week helped me realize that we needed to spend more time together and get to know each other. . . ."[20] Like the Trelease family, others seemed to discover also that a week without television was not the dreary, dull hardship they had envisioned. They learned by accident that a part of the media problem is not *what* children watch but *that* they watch television instead of doing other worthwhile things, like reading, helping out in the home or neighborhood, or developing their own talents and skills.[21]

As is true in every other aspect of character development, the parents' personal example is the most critical element in educating children about the proper place and use of the media. Parents who discriminate in their own viewing, who refuse to bring violent or obscene materials into their homes, who are willing to take a moral stand about what they see and hear, and who help their children develop responsible viewing habits greatly decrease the negative impact of the media.

Obviously, profits and the bottom line drive major media decisions. Regardless of the hype, movie makers will not continue to make movies which fail at the box office, and television executives cannot afford to produce shows which receive low ratings. They understand that they cannot sell what we refuse to buy. Consequently, we have to face the uncomfortable truth in the allegation that the entertainment industry gives the public what it wants.

They will push the limits just as far as we allow them to. Those who are guided by a very different agenda are imparting their values to our children, and they are presenting them in very attractive, seductive packaging. Those who care the most about children—their parents and teachers—have tended to take a more passive role, and we are now seeing the sad results. Now is the time to make our views known to legislators and to media executives and their sponsors, imploring them to take more responsibility for the media's influence on children. Until that happens, we need to remember that every TV set, VCR, and tape player has an off button. We simply must have the will and the courage to use it.

[1] The Associated Press, "Boy Says Violent Movie Inspired Shooting," Burlington (NC) *Times-News*, December 5, 1997.

[2] Fredric Wertham, "School for Violence, Mayhem in the Mass Media," *Where Do You Draw the Line?* Wicktor B. Cline, ed. (Provo, UT: Brigham Young University Press, 1974), p. 157.

[3] Neil Hickey, "The Experts Speak Out," *Violence on Television*, Editors of *TV Guide*, 1992, p. 4.

[4] Neil Hickey, op. cit., p. 2.

[5] Ibid.

[6] William Damon, *The Youth Charter: How Communities Can Work Together to Raise Standards for All Our Children* (New York: The Free Press, 1997), p. 147.

[7] Wayne Dosdick, *The Golden Rules: The Ten Ethical Values Parents Need to Teach Their Children* (San Francisco: HarperCollins Publishers, 1995), p. 152.

[8] Jeffrey L. Scheler, "Spiritual America," *U. S. News & World Report*, April 4, 1994, p. 57.

[9] Mortimer B. Zuckerman, "Where Have All the Values Gone? *U. S. News & World Report*, August 8, 1994, p. 88.

[10] Michael Medved, *Hollywood vs. America: Popular Culture and the War on Traditional Values* (New York: HarperCollins Publishers, 1992), p. 10.

[11] Sylvia Ann Hewlitt and Cornel West, *The War Against Parents* (Boston: Houghton Mifflin Company, 1998), p. 127.

[12] Michael Medved, op. cit., pp. 107-108.

[13] Media Violence Fact Sheet, *Beyond Blame: Challenging Violence in the Media*, (video program), Center for Media Literacy, 1995.

[14] Diane Levin, *Remote Control Childhood? Combating the Hazards of Media Culture* (Washington, DC: National Association for the Education of Young Children, 1998), p. 9.

[15] Thomas Lickona, *Educating for Character: How Our Schools Can Teach Respect and Responsibility* (New York: Bantam Books, 1992), p. 406.

[16] Diane Levin, op. cit.

[17] Judith Myers-Walls, "Suggestions for Parents: Children Can Unlearn Violence," *Media & Values*, Summer, 1993, p. 19.

[18] Jim Trelease, *The New Read-Aloud Handbook* (New York: Penguin Books, 1989), p. 130.

[19] Michael Ryan, "Are You Ready for TV-Turnoff Week?" *Parade Magazine*, April 12, 1998, pp. 16-17.

[20] Marie Winn, *Unplugging the Plug-in Drug* (New York: Viking Penguin, 1987), p. 156.

[21] Thomas Lickona, *Raising Good Children* (New York: Bantam Books, 1994), p. 358.

Remember that you are the adult!

T he youth was seventeen, and many of his friends were getting tattoos. He decided that he wanted one too, so he waged a vigorous campaign for almost a year, trying to persuade his mother to sign the required permission form. She refused. The son increased the pressure, reasoning that he would soon be a man and was quite capable of making adult decisions by himself. Retaining her parental authority, his mother held firm. As soon as he turned eighteen, he took advantage of his new adult status and went out and got a tattoo. His mother, although not happy about his decision, asked to see the results. Expecting to see some symbol of masculinity, she was surprised at what she saw: an image of Mickey Mouse!

Anyone who has worked with youth either in the home or in schools can appreciate this anecdote from a recent *Reader's Digest.* It reminds us that children and teenagers are a strange, touching blend of childishness and autonomy. Both qualities are normal as they advance from the total dependence of childhood to the independence and maturity of adulthood. One moment they move us to tears with their wisdom and concern for others; then, in the twinkling of an eye, they revert to very childlike and often childish behavior. These shifts in mood and maturity often surprise even the youths themselves, and it is a struggle sometimes for the adults in their world not to get hooked into some immature words and deeds of their own.

Rudyard Kipling's classic poem *If* summarizes strength of character and identifies several tests of maturity. The beginning lines "*If you can keep your head when all about you / are losing theirs and blaming it on you*" take on special meaning in the daily interactions in the home and family. Keeping one's head, modeling self-control, and treating others with respect are truly tested when interacting with children or teenagers who are angry, tired, frustrated, or confused. The daunting challenge is to listen to their concerns without being infected by them and to respond with reasoned guidance and direction.

A successful teacher once told me that the most helpful advice she received as a young educator was to always remember when interacting with children and youth that *one of you has to be an adult*. Later, when she had children of her own, she often remembered that advice—especially when they became teenagers. For her, recalling those simple words helped to defuse many tense moments in the home and in the classroom. She learned early in her career that children have lots of friends, and they don't really need another playmate or buddy, especially one of the older generation. They may even resent the grown-up "wannabes" who attempt to look, act, talk, and dress like them. What children desperately need, even when they can't articulate it, are adults at home and at school who are able and willing to serve as moral mentors and guides.

To illustrate, picture the following scene: Your elementary-age children are playing in the family room, and you are reading the newspaper nearby. The children have a disagreement; the argument escalates. Finally, one of the children loses his temper, raises his voice, and uses profanity. (We understand, of course, that the child learned those words somewhere else!) The children know that you heard the comment. What is their first reaction? If they are at all typical, they will immediately look at you. For a split-second, they freeze. Everything stops because they want to know how *you* are going to react and what *you* are going to do.

Likewise, consider another situation. A high school sophomore is talking to a group of his peers. He describes his weekend adventures that led to his wrecking the family car and receiving a ticket for speeding and careless and reckless driving. Temporarily, the youth is the center of attention, and his friends listen with intent interest. The other youths might joke, tease, or experience vicarious excitement, but the odds are very good that one of their first questions will be "What did your parents say?" or "What did your dad do?"

The reason for these initial reactions is that children and youth *expect* adults to be the moral authorities in their lives. They might overlook, accept, or even defend inappropriate behavior from their peers, but they hold their parents, teachers, and other adults to a higher standard. Beyond that, they *need* the security of knowing that there are some things that we believe in strongly, that we are willing to defend. When parents fail to do that, when they assume a neutral moral position or violate the principles of character they have attempted to teach their children, they lose credibility. At the same time, they communicate the cynical message that no principles *really* matter to them.[1]

There are many approaches to the guidance and discipline of children, but most of them fall into one of three broad categories: *permissive, autocratic,* or *authoritative.* It is natural for young teachers and parents to want to be loved and to be popular. The easy, short-term way to do that is to be very *permissive,* simply let children have their way, and allow them to have or do whatever they wish. Predictably, children reared in such a manner never really develop self-discipline, responsibility or true respect for themselves or others. They typically become selfish and self-centered and have little regard for authority in the home, the school or the community. When something happens, they look to their parents to excuse or to rescue them and to share their belief that if they fail, surely someone else is to blame.

On the other hand, some parents who recognize the risks in this approach, swing to the other extreme and become overly harsh and punitive. They set strict, rigid standards for their children's conduct and assume a "do it because I said so" attitude. Rather than using reasonable standards of behavior to help children develop good character, they seek obedience just for the sake of obedience and control. Their children typically obey out of fear, and they may become resentful of all authority and rebel when they finally manage to break free of their parents' control. This *autocratic* manner usually results in compliance, but it does not really build self-discipline or a desire to behave in a responsible, respectful, and caring manner just because it is the right and moral thing to do.

A third approach—the *authoritative* approach—provides greater balance than either permissive or autocratic parenting. In the home and in the school, the use of reasoned, legitimate adult authority gives children a sense of security and predictability. It gives children the assurance that someone who has their interest at heart is in control of the home and family. In *Beyond the Classroom: Why School Reform Has Failed and What Parents Need to Do*, Laurence Steinberg describes authoritative homes as those in which parents are "warm, firm and supportive" of their children's developing autonomy.[2] They set reasonable standards for their children, and they take seriously their responsibility for modeling responsible, mature behavior.

Authoritative parents don't hesitate to make their views and expectations known, but they also talk with and listen to their children. Like the mother who didn't want someone else deciding whether her children would participate in a particular activity, authoritative parents willingly take responsibility for their decisions regarding their children. In short, they are firm but fair, and they establish their roles as soon as their children are old enough to understand. They refuse to trade their legitimate, long-term parental authority for fleeting moments of popularity with their children and their peers. Perhaps more important, they are willing to endure periods of anger and rejection when it is in the best interest of their children, even though it would be easier to simply give in to their children's requests or to ignore their inappropriate behavior.

Not surprisingly, children reared by authoritative parents are generally more successful in school than those who grow up in more permissive or more autocratic homes.[3] Why is this? First, because they have learned to accept responsibility for their own actions, they are more psychologically mature. They are willing to work hard, to persist, and to make the necessary effort to succeed academically. Because they have had opportunities to face and meet challenges at home, they know the joy of tackling a difficult task and doing it well. They are more self-reliant than those raised in permissive homes where little is expected of them or those whose autocratic parents control everything they do.

A second reason children whose parents are authoritative tend to achieve greater academic success is that they have a "healthy attributional style." That is, they take responsibility for their own scholastic success or failure. If they do not do well in school, they attribute it to their own lack of effort rather than blaming someone else. If they are successful, they view their success as the result of their hard work and diligence. Because they make the connection between their efforts and their academic success, children of authoritative parents seem to "feel more confident that they—not their teachers, their genes , or the luck of the draw—control their fate."[4]

That scholastic confidence is reflected in other areas of youngsters' lives. If their parents serve as moral guides, they are much more likely *to learn* and *to live* principles of character such as respect, honesty, responsibility, and compassion. Clearly, adults have awesome power to influence youngsters' lives for good or ill, as Dr. Haim Ginott learned as a young teacher. He summarized that power as follows:

> I've come to a frightening conclusion. I am the decisive element in the classroom. It's my personal approach that creates the climate. It's my daily mood that makes the weather. As a teacher, I possess tremendous power to make a child's life miserable or joyous. I can be a tool of torture or an instrument of inspiration. I can humiliate or humor, hurt or heal. In all situations, it is *my* response that decides whether a crisis will be escalated or de-escalated and a child humanized or dehumanized.[5]

Whether we are teachers in the classroom or in the home, we have that same capacity to affect the climate in a child's world. Our conduct is critical because children and teenagers are taking their cues from the adults around them. The way we handle seemingly ordinary situations and interactions can have a lasting impact on the kind of people they will become. They expect us to keep our head when "all about us are losing theirs," and they are looking to us for models of responsible adulthood and good character.

[1] William Damon, *The Youth Charter: How Communities Can Work Together to Raise Standards for All Our Children* (New York: The Free Press, 1997), p. xii.

[2] Laurence Steinberg, *Beyond the Classroom: Why School Reform Has Failed and What Parents Need to Do* (New York: Simon & Schuster, 1996), p. 123.

[3] Steinberg, op. cit.

[4] Ibid.

[5] Haim Ginott, *Teacher and Child: A Book for Parents and Teachers* (New York: Avon Books, 1972), p. 13.

Conclusion

I T WAS THE BEST OF TIMES, it was the worst of times, it was the age of wisdom, it was the age of foolishness, it was the epoch of belief, it was the epoch of incredulity, it was the season of Light, it was the season of Darkness, it was the spring of hope, it was the winter of despair.

These opening lines from *A Tale of Two Cities* could well describe our own era. During the nine months I have been writing this book, I have seen examples of both extremes. On the one hand, a monumental scandal involving the President of the United States has stunned the nation. The nightly news is filled with accounts of improper behavior at the highest levels. There are also continuing reports of violence, especially among the young, and yet another television season has begun, with more of the same irreverence and disrespect that we have seen before.

On the other hand, during that same time period, issues such as morality, decency, honesty, and faithfulness have made their way into daily conversations. News commentators, editorial writers, and the man and woman on the street are openly addressing character issues and the importance of positive family values. Many schools and churches across America are renewing their efforts to teach children—directly and deliberately—to "know the good, to love the good, and to do the good." In short, we as a nation are now seeing the folly of thirty years of moral relativism and are starting to understand that there are some basic principles of character which are timeless and that they must be taught to each new generation.

As I talk with parents in my own community and in other parts of the nation, I sense a deep concern for their children and the messages our youth are receiving in today's society. In other words, there seems to be a growing *will*—both in the home and in the larger society—to take steps to counteract some of the negativism and violence in our world. The slogan *"children are always the only future the human race has; teach them well"* seems to have taken on new meaning and new relevance.

During World War II, four chaplains—two Protestant ministers, one Catholic priest, and a Jewish rabbi—were on the troop ship *Dorchester*. When the ship was torpedoed off the coast of Greenland, these four men gave up their own life jackets so that others might survive. When last seen, they were on the deck of the ship, singing hymns as it sank. This story of heroism is familiar and touching. Less well known is that one of the chaplains had written a letter to his wife and family several months earlier in which he said, "War is a dangerous business. Please do not pray that God will only keep me safe. Pray that God will make me adequate."[1]

Just as those chaplains demonstrated the triumph of the human spirit, we, too, can make a difference in the world. By our overt teaching, by our involvement of youth in positive activities, and by our daily efforts to model good behavior, I believe that we *can* increase the likelihood that today's children will grow up to be good and caring adults. And as we—parents, teachers, and members of the faith community—work together to help our youth become people of good character, my prayer is that God will make us adequate to the task.

[1] Jack Hunter, "Steeple Talk," Burlington (NC) *Times News*, July 31, 1993.

THE GOLDEN RULE

Christianity
Do unto others as you would have them do unto you.

Judaisim
What is hateful to you, do not do to your fellow man.
That is the entire law. All the rest is commentary.

Buddhisim
Hurt not others in ways that you yourself would find
hurtful.

Islam
No one of you is a believer until he desires for his brother
that which he desires for himself.

Hinduism
Do nothing to thy neighbor which thou wouldst not have
him do to thee thereafter.

Baha'i Faith
Blessed is he who preferreth his brother before himself.

Confucianism
What you do not want done to yourself, do not do to others.

Reading and Resource List for Parents.

Bennett, William J. *The Book of Virtues.* New York: Simon & Schuster, 1993.

Bennett, William J. *The Book of Virtues for Children.* New York: Simon & Schuster, 1995.

Bennett, William J. *The Book of Virtues for Young People.* , NJ: Silver Burdett Press, 1996.

Bennett, William J. *The Moral Compass.* New York: Simon & Schuster, 1995.

Coles, Robert. *The Moral Intelligence of Children.* New York: Random House, 1997.

Damon, William. *The Youth Charter: How Communities Can Work Together to Raise Standards for All Our Children.* New York: The Free Press, 1997.

Dosdick, Wayne. *Golden Rules: The Ten Ethical Values Parents Need to Teach Their Children.* San Francisco: Harper Collins Publishers, 1995.

Hunt, Gladys. *Honey for a Child's Heart.* Grand Rapids, MI: Zondervan Publishing House, 1989.

Kilpatrick, William. *Why Johnny Can't Tell Right from Wrong.* New York: Simon & Schuster, 1992.

Kilpatrick, William and Gregory and Suzanne M. Wolfe. *Books*

That Build Character. New York: Simon & Schuster, 1994.

Levin, Diane E. *Remote Control Childhood? Combating the Hazards of Media Culture*. Washington, DC: National Association for the Education of Young Children, 1998.

Lickona, Thomas. *Educating for Character: How Our Schools Can Teach Respect and Responsibility*. New York: Bantam Books, 1992.

Lickona, Thomas. *Raising Good Children*. New York: Bantam Books, 1994.

Napier, Kristine. *The Power of Abstinence*. New York: Avon Books, 1994.

Rosemond, John. *Six-Point Plan for Raising Happy, Healthy Children*. Kansas City: Andrews and McMeel, 1997.

Trelease, Jim. *The Read-Aloud Handbook, 4th Edition*. New York: Penguin Books, 1995.

Vincent, Philip Fitch. *Developing Character in Students: A Primer for Teachers, Parents and Communities*. Chapel Hill: Character Development Publications, 1994.

Vincent, Philip Fitch, Editor. *Promising Practices in Character Education: Nine Success Stories from Around the Country*. Chapel Hill: Character Development Group, 1996.

ORDER FORM

Book Title

Book Title	Quantity	Price	Total
ADVISOR/ADVISEE CHARACTER EDUCATION *24 Lessons to Develop Character in Students*, S. SADLOW		$24.95	
CHARACTER EDUCATION *Superintendent's & Administrator's Guide To...*, D. HODGIN		$3.95	
CHARACTER EDUCATION WORKBOOK *A "How-To" Manual for School Boards, Administrators & Community Leaders*, J. HOFFMAN & A. LEE		$12.00	
DEVELOPING CHARACTER IN STUDENTS *A Primer for Teachers, Parents & Communities*, P. VINCENT		$12.95	
JOURNEYS IN EDUCATION LEADERSHIP *Lessons From Eighteen Principals of the Year*, A. HART		$12.00	
LESSONS FROM THE ROCKING CHAIR *Timeless Stories For Teaching Character*, DEB BROWN		$6.00	
PARENTS, KIDS & CHARACTER *21 Strategies for Helping Your Children Develop Good Character*, H. LEGETTE		$15.95	
PROMISING PRACTICES IN CHARACTER EDUCATION *Nine Success Stories from Across the Country*, MULTIPLE		$12.00	
RULES AND PROCEDURES *The First Step Toward School Civility*, P. VINCENT		$14.00	
TEACHING CHARACTER *Teacher's Idea Book*, A. DOTSON & K. WISONT		$24.00	
Parent's Idea Book, A. DOTSON & K. WISONT		$12.00	

Subtotal

NC Tax (6%)

Shipping Total

Total

SHIPPING:
Up to $25 .... $4
$25 to $100 .... $6
Over $100 .... 6%

Form of payment: Check ☐   PO # ☐

Make checks payable to:
Character Development Publishing, PO Box 9211, Chapel Hill, NC 27515-9211

Ship To:

Name

Organization   Title

Address

City: State: Zip:

Phone: (   )   Signature:

FAX ORDERS: (919) 967-2139

For further information, or to schedule a Character Development Workshop, call **(919) 967-2110**, or e-mail to **Respect96@aol.com**
Visit our WebSite at **charactereducation.com**
(Call regarding quantity discounts) HL99

CHARACTER DEVELOPMENT GROUP

PO Box 9211
Chapel Hill, NC 27515

CHARACTER DEVELOPMENT GROUP offers complete resources, including publications and staff development training for the planning, implementation and assessment of an effective character education program in schools and school systems.